Law Enforcement Culture
UNVEILED

Officer Jim Banish

Law Enforcement Culture
UNVEILED

Jim Banish

© 2023
First Edition

**This work, and all of my work, is
dedicated to my brother Joey.**

This is the last photo ever taken of him.

May Joey's sacrifice
lead to the positive change we need
in law enforcement culture.

THE CHAPTERS

AN IMPULSIVE ACT

JOSEPH JAMES BANISH 'JOEY'

THE DOWNWARD SPIRAL

KEEPING PROMISES

THE ULTIMATE BETRAYAL

MY OWN DOWNWARD SPIRAL

I AM NOT ALONE

BLAME

WE USED TO BE HEROES

LAW ENFORCEMENT CULTURE

LEAPING FORWARD

ADVANCING THE TREATMENTS, PERFECTING THE PROGRAM

VALOR STATION

THE SAME DREAM

RESOURCES

FORWARD...

WE CAN ONLY GO FORWARD

Purpose. The most defining purposes in this life will always be born from the greatest whys. When our whys are teamed up with meaning, truth, and undeniable sincerity, our purpose will burn brightly until the day we take our last breath. It is then that the lives of those we touch are forever changed for the better, and when this comes to pass, our purpose surpasses our last breath.

It is curious how some can be knocked down by life, and stay down, while others can be knocked down by the same punch and bounce back from the depths of Hell's Gate and be better for it. While personalities and past experiences will be a factor, the key will always be in the work you do, post blast. We can be defined by our tragedies, or we can move on from them. We can perpetually live in trauma time, or we can do the work and get better. We can store "it" away in a box, never to be opened again, or we can snatch the box up from the deep and open it on our terms, on our playing field. For it is true that left unaddressed, and left unopened, the box will open itself on its own terms, ready or not. It's your choice.

Jim Banish has done the work, and then some. In the two years following Joe Banish's death, Jim's life was on the cruelest of rollercoaster rides. He not only lost his brother and best friend; he also experienced strained, even fractured relationships with his family. A family that, prior to April 1, 2008, set the bar. The quintessential, hard-working American family, that other families wished they could be. That was the Banish family. For two years, Jim was fatally paralyzed. Paralyzed with guilt, grief, depression, anxiety, and with a dim outlook for the future.

Then one day, Jim Banish got help. He sought out the help of a psychologist. How bad could one visit be? He was already living in Hell on earth, so what did he have to lose? The question would soon be reframed into a statement. It became what he stood to <u>gain</u> by seeking help. This was the day the seed was planted. This was the day that would slowly launch Jim into a space he would never imagine himself existing in before, and especially in the aftermath of April 1, 2008. It's basic math, I suppose. Brotherly love plus unwavering purpose equals saved lives, careers, marriages, and dreams. It's so simple, yet so complex. It's simple, as all our basic needs are the same, or so Maslow tells us. It's so complex, as we are all different and bring different experiences to the table. Despite the differences, though, we all appreciate and respond to a caring ear. We are grateful when a hand reaches out to us. We are all better when we are valued, appreciated, and know the meaning of our place in this world. In my professions as a state trooper or clinician, I have never witnessed a level of wholeheartedness in his approach to helping others as I have in Jim Banish. Whether it's at a Post Critical Incident Seminar, at a training session, a phone call at 3:00 AM, or in these pages you are about to read, you will see that Jim Banish was sent by God, with the high recommendation of Joe Banish. It's my honor to write this forward and a privilege to call Jim my friend and brother.

Andrew P. Carrier, LCSW, LISW-CP

THIS BOOK WILL SAVE LIVES.

AN IMPULSIVE ACT

The very word *suicide* makes people apprehensive, confused, sad, and wary of hearing the details. When traumatic, devastating events happen, you either remember everything or you block those details out completely. Somehow, when I lost my brother, I did both. I remember the horrific scene of his suicide vividly, fifteen years later. But the next day, driving to our parent's home, I can't tell you how I got there. Not much of that trip at all. My children were curled up on the back seat of the car and I just drove.

I wondered if such a reaction was dissociation; a way to remove myself mentally from a situation that was so appalling, so painful I could hardly even breathe, much less consider the future without my closest sibling. To this day, I don't recall much of that five hour drive. I was trying to figure out a hundred other things and my mind was still not believing that my mentor, my hero, my best friend, was gone. I could not believe that he would take his own life. Could I have stopped him? Could I have done something to ease his pain? We will never know and that is a burden I will always bear.

Suicide is often considered to be an impulsive act, to all of us it is a drastic decision. The deciding individual finally has had enough of this world and sees no other solution. As a society we are not completely sure what the motivators are because the people we would ask are no longer available for questioning. They are in your life and then they are gone. I was astonished, frankly. Suicide was what happened to other families. It didn't have a place in my stoic, stable, religious clan. Suicide was something that I never thought would encroach upon my world. No, that's not true; I never really thought about it at all, and now it impacts me every day of my life.

Members of Law Enforcement (LE) see the aftermath of these acts, and it's gut-wrenching. As an officer, I have performed many notifications about death; whether by suicide, homicide, or accident, and none of them are ever easy. I dutifully performed them much more often than I wanted to, and had probably become a bit callous, even, as that is what my career required; that is what my mind required. I have given people bad news about the people they loved more times than I can count and many more times than I care to remember.

The phone call to my mother telling her that her oldest son was gone was the hardest one I ever had to make. It changed my whole perspective. I am no longer callous, and I work every day to make sure those phone calls happen less often.

JOSEPH JAMES BANISH (JOEY)

My folks have been together fifty-four years. It's an impressive record and shows dedication to each other and to us, the five children that they raised and the grandchildren that they now adore. My dad was a military man and then a Judge for thirty-plus years, among other things. As kids we occasionally went to arraignments at night, which I found riveting and inspiring. As a family we followed his career and his way of thinking. We believed in justice. We believed in doing the right thing and punishing the guilty. Clearly that had a very profound impact on the adults that we became. All three sons entered law enforcement, the oldest, Joe, considered a law degree but at the last minute applied to the New York State Police Academy and passed the tests with flying colors. My younger brother Mike serves with the Virginia State Troopers. I started with New York State Law Enforcement when I was only twenty. We were the good guys, doing good things. Then Joe's arm of the law turned against him and he took his own life, with his service weapon, in full uniform, at age thirty-five.

We didn't have a truly typical childhood but it was a 'Mayberry' type of town in Western New York State near Buffalo. Not a whole lot of bad things happened there. Structure was predominant in our lives; we were raised in a strict household and taught that blood was thicker than water. Everything was black and white; to this day my father doesn't really show much emotion; he is this rock of a person. That's how I always think of him. He looked to the laws and rules of society, he set the tone, and we followed his lead. My father is a philosopher of sorts and my brother Mike is a carbon copy; he's very close to my parents, still attached at the cord, I like to say. He's had a lot of trauma, he lost his best friend in the line of duty, and then he lost his brother. Mike has served nineteen years and has not asked for any sort of outlet at this point; I think he will need it eventually. We all do. He'll know when he's ready.

My Mother is the nerve center of the family. She's a true Mom. Everybody gravitated to her, and she instilled in us that you always have time to help someone else. Joe especially took that lesson to heart. My older sister Jennifer is an elementary school teacher in the school we all graduated from, and loves her job after all these years and all these changes in education. For a while, she and my Mom worked in the same district. Jennifer was another mother hen and she helped raise the other four of us, it just made sense. My other sister Mary now directs a program for autistic children in Virginia. We are incredibly close-knit Catholics. I was an altar boy; we were the whole nine yards of conservative small-town life. It was a great childhood and probably, like many of you, I appreciate it much more now than I did then.

Joseph James Banish taking his life was not how this was supposed to turn out; we're cops, we're the good guys, we're the heroes. It wasn't until I became a cop that my world view was shattered and I learned how many assholes and criminals there are on the planet. I honestly experienced a huge feeling of moral injury. I didn't understand how shitty life could be, I had never seen it. The amount of trauma, sexual abuse, and violence is, quite simply, astonishing. Add in bullshit politics and no wonder this generation is fucked up. Childhood is no longer so beautiful, so innocent. It's no wonder we all have issues. If I didn't have such a strong upbringing, I probably wouldn't be here today.

A full four years older than me, Joe and I were incredibly close. We did everything together, even in high school he invited me along wherever he went. Joe looked out for all of us in a loving, not overbearing, sort of way. He had great grades, much better than me, and went to Saint Bonaventure University to study Pre-Law. I've always said that I went to college twice because even though I was so much younger he always included me in his world. I loved it. We were a team, although I was more of an athlete, and Joe was very cerebral, intelligent, and goal oriented. He excelled in everything. I'm sure I sound a little bias, because I'm very proud of my brother, but he truly did. He definitely excelled within the New York State Police.

After New York Troopers graduate the Academy in Albany, the State Police sends a lot of those rookies north, to B Troop, up by the Canadian border. I was in Florida having a blast checking out the beaches, the bikinis, and the beer, while trying to be a pro baseball player. I was good enough for Western New York but I wasn't good enough for the Major Leagues; that reality had set in and I was looking for my next step. When Joe got stationed up north he decided I should join him. I wasn't absolutely sure about it, but because he asked, I made the decision to move in with him in Westport, New York and attend Clinton Community College, then eventually the State University of New York (SUNY) at Plattsburgh.

We were poor, really poor. They didn't pay Troopers all that much at the turn of the century and it was a paltry sum thirty years ago. We barely had enough money to survive with me going to school. The winters up in the North Country are nearly unbearable and our heat was so expensive that we lived in a very cold apartment. We had one heated blanket. Only one. He often worked nights and I went to school days so when he came home he just crawled into the warm bed and I went on my way. Many cold nights we slept in the same bed to stay warm and would stay up late talking about our childhood and even our future plans. Joe and I were so close that was just a normal deal for us. We shared blankets and a philosophy on the world, always taking care of each other. We faced challenges in similar ways, although he was the thinker and I was much more mechanical.

I need to give you an example of the kind of guy Joe was, even though these stories sometimes bring me to tears. "Grab your tools," he said to me one morning, bursting into my room. It was February, way below zero, and some family had broken down on the Northway. The Northway is Interstate 87, which is pretty much the only road from New York City to Canada. I told him he was crazy, but I already knew we were going to go help. "You gotta fix the car so they can get home," he said to me, grabbing my clothes. Turned out this car was some piece of shit Chevy, all rusted out, and the alternator had died. I was working on it, freezing my ass off, while they sat in the warm car and Joe got to know this guy. It was Sunday and of course there were no parts stores open, so we drove the forty-something miles to the next town, got the part, and the man told my brother that he couldn't afford to pay for it. Let me tell you that Joe couldn't afford that part either but paid for it anyway, I put it in, and we told him not to worry about the cost. Joe had even put the family up in a little hotel because it was so cold. The man never paid him back, never even contacted him. Joe didn't care about that. He simply never wanted to see anyone in need, he was always there for people.

He and I had a very simple life back then; we had great times. We were a team, closer than ever. Even as a rookie, Joe knew that his goal was to be the Superintendent of the State Police, the head honcho. That was his dream, although I may be the only one who ever knew he had such high aspirations. He had decided to do whatever it took to succeed.

Predictably enough, Joe was thinking I needed to succeed as well. I was twenty at the time, and really just having a blast without any true direction, working at a golf course, coming home late, unable to decide what was next for me. I hadn't thought too much about the future and I definitely wasn't focused on a career in law enforcement. Joe decided for me. He contacted the Police Academy in Western New York and got me in, just like that, in 1997. I passed all the tests and I guess I liked it well enough. Here I am, Sheriff's Officer Jim Banish, twenty-five years later, telling my story. Back then law enforcement was a very respected career with good benefits, a practical choice to work with good people. To 'Serve and Protect.' I know that my brother was passionate about his calling and thought he was doing the best thing for me, too, leading me down a similar path.

During his fifteen years of service, Joe moved anytime the state wanted him to; he worked in every Troop except one and I think the constant transitions cost him a great relationship. He had a woman that wanted to marry him but he chose his career, and transferred with one of his promotions instead of staying with her. I have to be honest about this; he was so handsome and charming that he recovered very quickly and always had a girl or two on the line somewhere, but he never did marry and never got over that long relationship; it was like nobody could measure up to her. A lot of the guys called him 'Trooper Chippendale', or 'Hollywood', and when he was stationed out there he was the 'Long Island Lolita'. Everybody knew about Joey; he was the poster child of the NYS Police. He went to the gym, was very fit and always perfectly groomed; he had a great presence, an impeccable record and a rock-star smile.

Only a few years into his career he sat for the Sergeant's exam and passed, becoming the youngest ever at the time. He enjoyed his time as a Sergeant but knew it was only a stepping stone for his career. He opted for a lateral move within the agency to investigator and got stationed at the Casino in Niagara Falls, New York; it was during this time that he was prepping and studying for his next step up the ladder. Joe took the next promotional exam, for Lieutenant, when he had been on the force about ten years, which is very unusual. He studied like a maniac for six months; he was meticulous about it. He would record himself reading the manual, ask himself questions, and play them back in the car on one of those old school tape recorders that most kids now wouldn't even recognize! That's how obsessed he was at being the best, following the rules, doing the right thing. It all paid off. He scored #7 on the list, one of the youngest ever to do that well. There are over five thousand State Troopers in New York and my brother was climbing that ladder like few ever had.

Meanwhile, the now-Lieutenant Banish kept looking after people, even when his peers weren't looking out for him. There was this janitor at the academy, (I guess you have to call them Sanitation Engineers or something now to be politically correct), and he was a special needs guy. Most of the Troopers laughed and made fun of him but Joey didn't pick on him. He took him to the gym on his lunch break, taught him to work out, took the time to treat him like a person. Joe was that guy. Truth be told, that man cried outright when he heard that my brother was gone. He, too, knew it was a great loss.

Joe never forgot where he came from, never forgot what his mother had taught him, that no individual is more valuable than another and that everyone deserves to be treated fairly. As a Lieutenant, in 2007, he took a position at the New York State Police Academy as an administrator and was incredibly excited about the opportunity. Incredibly proud. I told you his goal; he wanted to have a huge impact on the future of the New York State Police, to make them better. His plan was going great up to this point. He knew he needed to train the cadets differently in these changing times. If anyone could have done it, let me tell you, it was Joe.

THE DOWNWARD SPIRAL

The changes came later that very same year, 2007. I noticed them first after he had been at the Academy for just a few months. The differences got progressively more obvious. We had many conversations regarding his role at the academy and also the stressors of being a Lieutenant there. It was at this point that he started to mention that the NYSP wasn't exactly what he thought it would be, and being a Lieutenant exposed him to some of the darker sides of the agency and even some backstabbing and betrayal. I also noticed that he was drinking more often and even eating less. A few months later the family gathered for Christmas as always and Joe was distant, definitely not himself. Prior to this, when he walked into a room, he lit it up, and that was no longer the case. Joey went off by himself that afternoon, which was very rare, especially on a holiday. I looked for him and found him in the dark with a beer, just staring off into space. I asked if he was okay and he told me he had a lot going on, lots of politics, he called it, and explained that he was just stressed out. He eventually re-engaged with the family but I took note and as I watched him that day, I started thinking there must have been a whole lot more to it.

A few weeks later I invited him to my place for the annual Daytona 500 Race, which is always on Sunday, ordered a pizza, grabbed some beer. I had planned some alone time with him, which is really what I wanted. I know this may be unnecessary detail but you have to understand how shocked I was; I can picture these moments like they were yesterday. We were enjoying each other's company like we always had, eating the pie and downing a couple beers. I got up to go to the bathroom and when I returned, I stepped down onto the landing in the living room and stopped in my tracks. Joe was sitting on the couch by the big stone fireplace, staring off into space. I saw tears running down his face; he was crying. I was stunned, shocked, speechless. I'd never seen that, in all our years together. My family, especially the men in my family, don't cry. We just don't. Well, let me amend that; we never used to.

I didn't know what to do so I made a little noise to warn him that I was returning to the room. He looked at me and wiped his eyes. There was such sorrow written all over his face it tore at my heart. I sat across the coffee table, looked right into his eyes and asked him what the hell was going on. He told me it was from smoke; he had put a log on the fire, and that he was okay. "Bullshit, I've never seen you like this," I told him straight out. "You're scaring the shit out of me." I really was frightened to my very core. He fessed up that things at work were very 'uncomfortable,' and that turned out to be quite an understatement.

Joe had changed, those last few months, both physically and mentally, there was no doubt about that. He knew it too, and that day, finally, he took me into his confidence. He had disagreed with his fellow officers on the disciplinary action of a superior, a Major. I won't relay the full details about the situation, but it was a very big deal and after that Joe had enemies. He was living in a culture where people did not defy the norms. They went along with the crowd, whether they agreed with it or not, whether it was right or not. Administrative betrayal, I call it now. "It's just not what I thought it was going to be," he told me sadly. His story took over three and a half hours that day; he was unburdened, but it wasn't enough.

After that refusal to conform, Joey had the bullseye on him, so to speak, and another officer added even more fuel to the fire. If you're stationed at the Academy, you stay in barracks-style housing, similar to a dormitory. As a Lieutenant, Joe had his own room, went out one night, and brought a lady back with him. A fellow officer filed a personnel complaint against him because he had an "unauthorized individual" on the grounds after hours. I'm told that the accuser herself had brought other people into her room, recruits even, and it's very common knowledge she had regularly broken that same rule. Everybody did. It was, and still is, in all probability, a common practice at the Academy.

As I understand the situation the accuser called Joe out for her own personal gain because she was looking to get promoted and wanted Joe's position. Publicly, he was being charged with the irrelevant, ridiculous, demeaning crime of having an unauthorized person visiting him in his Academy barracks room at age thirty-five. Privately, he was distraught, his illusion and dreams shattered just like my world view had been. These people are adults, after all, and while it was the rule of law, it was very rarely, if ever, enforced until this time. Formal charges were brought against Joe in January of 2008. Personnel complaints are a very serious deal in the State Police and are taken to Internal Affairs. So the conflict and the controversy began.

I have seen similar treatment of officers both prior to and since Joey's suicide. I will never be able to wrap my mind around how law enforcement can treat each other like this: the bullshit, the betrayal. There are many, many officers out there that are willing to step on you for their own gain or to move up the ranks, and in general it's an accepted practice. Quite frankly it makes me very angry and I've fought for officers time and time again because I know what can happen to them if they think they are all alone in a fight that they perceive as unwinnable. Let me tell you, it's disastrous.

I told you that Joe literally memorized the rule books, the manuals, the regulations and the procedures of the New York State Police so you know that he took his responsibilities very, very seriously. Did he know he was breaking a rule? Certainly, yes. It happened to be a rule that was disregarded by the entire organization; that was the way it had always been done, as long as anyone can remember.

However, when the situation arrived that a formal complaint was filed in regard to a formal rule of the same organization, it's a mess, right? And when the accuser is commonly known to have broken that rule as well, it gets even messier. She was eventually ostracized and retired, but not before the damage to Joe was done and she had successfully taken my brother's position after causing his death. In my estimation, that was a huge 'Fuck You' to my family. This is where Joe's downward spiral escalated. They were threatening him with demotion, even threatened to fire him. It didn't correlate, didn't make any sense, and I have always wondered if there are chapters of the story that have never been told. I could hardly believe what I was hearing.

In general, New York State Police Internal Affairs (IA) is nuts. I know that's not a particularly professional way to describe part of an organization, but it's appropriate. The system doesn't work. Let's just say you may get a slap on the wrist, three days off, or outright fired, you don't have any idea which it will be. As an officer, you just have to fester for several months to several years until they go through the process and you get an answer about your future, your livelihood, your life. IA has carte blanche, that's all there is. They are trying to torture their own, I swear; it's all about having power over people. It's reprehensible. I've seen it happen over and over. And this time it was my brother who was under the gun. They basically have unlimited power with very few checks and balances. Most people in New York don't even know that they are allowed to perform warrantless wiretaps, among other things. This is way too much power to go unchecked and they will use it to punish their own people when they feel it necessary or if, perhaps, you have gone against the grain.

KEEPING PROMISES

At my house that February day in front of a roaring fire, Joey bared his soul, and that's where the promises came in. He asked me to not tell anyone what was happening to him. He asked me to promise, even though it goes against all the core values of our family, our little tribe. I had trouble, I really did, but he was my favorite, my soul mate, so I promised my big brother that I would not share his secrets with anyone. In turn, he promised me that he would not hurt himself. It was the first time I ever put Joey and suicide into the same thought, but I had this crazy feeling that he just might make a bad decision and do himself harm. He promised me that he wouldn't. He promised. It was a promise he wouldn't live up to.

"Don't you have anyone to talk to?" I asked him. "Anything I say will create a stigma," he told me. "I'll be weak, I can't talk to them." He trusted no one. I knew the NYSP had an EAP program with peers to assist officers going through troubled times, so I asked Joey to maybe talk to one of them. He was adamant that he wouldn't talk to anyone and more specifically anyone from the New York State Police. He didn't trust them, and why should he? They had already turned on him. As the weeks went on, I talked to a local counselor and asked her to see him, as a favor. Honestly, what I needed was someone to tell me he was okay. She said she'd meet with him off the record, and he finally agreed. He wanted no one to know what was going on. A week went by, the day came. He called me and canceled. "I don't trust it; I don't need to tell anyone. It's a bad idea, Jim." "We need to figure out what's going on with you," I replied. "I'll go talk to my priest instead," he told me. "Jimmy, I'm not coming. I'll let you know how it goes."

Joe believed he would be letting my parents down if anything disciplinary happened, especially a demotion, especially over something so trivial and for doing nothing more than what others do within that agency. He was so prideful; he would not have been able to handle it; he would be letting himself down most of all. He called it politics but it was and is much more than that. At that time, law enforcement was a culture where you could not show emotion or weakness, even to save yourself. A culture where the majority rules. A culture that makes actions perfectly acceptable, maybe even celebrated, as long as it's always been done that way. Even if it's wrong. There is brotherhood and also betrayal. There is contradiction.

That spring I was ten years in, working and living not far from the Academy and I used to take a lot of what LE calls Prisoner Transports, which, under contract, take prisoners who are sentenced to terms longer than a year from local jails to state prison. I opted for the transports as often as I could just so I could go through Albany and see Joey. That's how connected we were. On April 1, 2008 I called him at 6:30am, from the locker room at work as I was putting my uniform on, to make sure we could meet for our usual lunch. When he answered he sounded groggy, which was really unusual; he said hadn't slept the night before. "I can't today," he told me. "I'm putting together a conference in Lake George; I can't meet you."

That was a huge red flag for me, because he never turned me down. Ever. Somehow, we always made it happen. I offered to drive up to Lake George, I was so looking forward to seeing him, I knew somehow that it was important to see him. He turned me down. Flag. Big red flag, but I still didn't understand what was happening. Because this was Joe. We ended our brief conversation by telling each other we loved one another.

I texted him twice on the road and received no response, which is also very unusual. I received a call from his girlfriend, who had not heard from him either and was checking with me. He had told her he would be busy, but we grew more and more concerned. After receiving no text replies, I called him a few times; no answer. Red flags. Not knowing what else to do, I started home with my mind spinning, focused on Joey. Half an hour later, his girlfriend called, completely incoherent, "Joey's here, I'm home, he shot himself." She was screaming, crying, panicked, horrified. I told her to call 911 and see if they could save him, and she did. I think we both knew that they couldn't.

I whipped the car around at some illegal U-turn intersection and headed to his house, my heart pounding. I called my mom on the way. She was in school, headed to her next class, focused on her day. "Jimmy, what'd you do now?" she asked, half joking; I was the one that was always in trouble, the wild card, the unpredictable son. "I didn't do anything, Mom. I need you to sit down and listen to me." Somehow it was important to me that she was sitting, that she could take the news. "I'm in a hurry, what is it?" she asked me. My sister, who at that time taught in the same elementary school (I told you this was a close-knit family) happened to walk in between her own classes. These things happen for a reason. "I know you're in a hurry," I insisted, "Just let me know when you're both sitting down." Finally, I think she sat, maybe they both did. I took a deep breath and said something I could never have imagined saying. "Mom, I don't know how to tell you this, but I just got a call from Joe's girlfriend; he went home for lunch and shot himself. That's all I know right now." I could hear her start to cry. She said, "Jimmy get there as fast as you can and promise me you'll do everything you can to help him until I get there. I will take care of him for the rest of his life if he needs that. Just get there." And that's exactly what I did.

There were already a slew of police cars, what we call brass, parked in front of Joe's place and all along the street. Scared beyond belief,

I parked on the neighbor's lawn and came face to face with ten or so officers, all high rank. They asked me who I was and I didn't have time for that; I honestly thought, or rather hoped, there still might be a chance that Joey was alive, that he might have somehow survived. I pushed past them, "Excuse me, I have to go." They told me I couldn't go in, even after I told them he was my brother. "I made a promise to my mom, and she outranks you." I told them. "I need to see my brother." There wasn't much questioning after that, but they were damn apprehensive about letting me through, and sent an investigator in with me.

I'll never forget what I walked into, and I wish I could. When I saw Joey, he was in full uniform, impeccable as always, shoes shined, the whole bit. He had put his service weapon to his head in his own living room and pulled the trigger. A rosary, notes, photos and personal items he had collected were on the couch. There was nothing that could be done to save him, that was perfectly clear. All I could do was say goodbye. I walked back outside and dialed my mom. She was still crying. I could hear an engine racing in the background, so I asked them to slow down. "There's nothing I can do, nothing any of us can do," I told them, "Joey's gone. Slow down."

After they took him away, we cleaned up the house; it was one of the worst things I've ever been tasked to do. I didn't want anyone else to remember him that way. When we got through, there were just a few stains on the couch and the ragged hole in the wall; the bullet had gone all the way through. We had pulled out the area rug, it was a pool of blood. As I told you, I can still picture the whole horrific scene, fifteen years later. I'm sure it will never go away.

After that, all I can remember is not knowing what to say or what to do. I had maintained an exterior calm and arranged for my family to meet at a hotel nearby. My sister and brother had come up from Virginia immediately, of course, because that is what we do, we support each other. My parents wanted to stay in my room; I'm certain they wanted time with me to find out more information about what had happened, and of course why it had happened. I told them what I knew, what he had been going through, the betrayal of his own people. The angst. They had no idea. I told them about the promises.

The next morning my Mom got in the shower early; she wanted to go see Joe. And then my father got in the shower, and for the first time, the only time ever, I heard that rock-like man cry. It was a desolate wailing, really, a terrible, sorrowful, sound. I was lying there in bed, thinking that my whole world was uprooted in one single pull of a trigger, six pounds of pressure changed everything. I dragged the blankets over my head, and just laid there, numb. I still have never told him what I heard that morning. To me, it was like a piece of steel cracking, splitting apart, giving way. All these years, I never told him. It shattered my soul. If my unshakeable father was crying I didn't think that any of us had a chance at a normal life any more. If it was that bad, how could the world even keep spinning? I couldn't have imagined anything being awful enough to induce my father to cry. I finally pulled the blankets down, stood in that same shower, and faced the second worst day of my life.

We went to Albany Medical Center, to the morgue, to see my big brother Joe. They had done as good a job as they possibly could cleaning him up for this moment, but it was still awful to see him lying on that stainless steel table. "I need a piece of my son," my mom asked them, "Is there anything I can have?" They denied her. It was absurd and appalling that they wouldn't give her anything. She asked for his watch. He always wore a watch on his right hand. They would not let her have it. It was crazy. Who makes those kind of rules? It was evidence, it was an investigation, they told us. There was nothing to investigate, that much was perfectly clear. This 'case' was cut and dry and done. Why should she be made to suffer by people who follow rules only when it's convenient?

My family regrouped, dreading the next step; we came up with a practical and awful plan; my stomach tightens when I think of this time. As reasonable, responsible people do, everyone went in different directions, to gather whatever needed to be gathered, and then we were to meet at my parent's house so we could bury one of the people we loved the most. I went and gathered my children to take them to my brother's funeral. It was surreal.

I dreaded telling ten-year-old Domanic, my oldest son, and Joey's special nephew, for a myriad of reasons. Ever since he was born it was a little bit of a family joke. Even when he was very young, my son looked like Joe and acted like Joe, so we teased that maybe he really was Joey's son, all in good fun. There was a very special bond between my brother and Domanic. For his tenth birthday gift, he desperately wanted a BB gun and Joe and I disagreed on that. I didn't want him to have a gun, not yet, of any sort. Joey decided it was time and gave it to him anyway. They shot for hours and hours that night. I don't know exactly how genetics work in a family, but I do know Domanic looks *exactly* like my brother Joe, to this day. If you're spiritual like I am, you have to think that Joe lives on, somehow, between what I'm doing and the legacies he left behind.

When I got to the house I went up to his bedroom, where he was curled up with a migraine. I knelt beside him, and told him his Uncle had been shot. I remember him sitting up and saying --"I'm not going to see Uncle Joe anymore?" I can still hear his voice. "Uncle Joe's dead," I told him. "And we're going to help Grandma now, so we gotta go." It was pretty awful, just like the rest of my day. With the resilience of a child, he got up, packed his bag, and came with me. Like a little soldier, like the little soldier that Joe would have wanted him to be. "Be strong," I told him. And he was. We packed a bag for my younger son, Jarrett, age five, my stepchildren Haley, Coby, and Riley also, and headed to my own childhood home.

That's when I took my unremembered drive across most of New York State. Some Trooper I didn't know ended up pulling me over, ironically enough, for speeding. I told him who I was and where I was going, so he let me go. I was indescribably sad and it was obvious that he was, too. He put his head down and told me he was sorry, that he had worked with Joey and couldn't believe it. No one could believe it.

THE ULTIMATE BETRAYAL

On the day of Joe's funeral, no one in the family could speak except my Mom. My brother and I were in full uniform, and I knew I couldn't even form coherent words, much less sentences. I have complete admiration that she had that much strength and courage. It was unprecedented, she is tough as nails. All she said was, "Well, Joey would have done that for me." And he would have. Officers showed up even though their time was not paid. The funeral was not part of the normal line of duty ceremonies because it was a suicide. Hundreds honored him as they would any other death, as we expected them to. Joe was special.

During the setup, I remember asking the Major who was in charge of the ceremony, "At what point do we have a flag on the coffin so it can be presented to my mom and dad?" He told me that the rule was there were no flags allowed for suicides; another betrayal, this one after his death. Only those officers killed *in* the line of duty were honored with a flag. Joe died *because* of the line of duty. The State Police, who Joseph James Banish had given fifteen years of his young life to, would not allow our national flag to drape his coffin. My parents were so shocked. I had to create a private ceremony and fold a flag for them, and I will never forget that. The New York State Police did not look particularly kindly on suicide, although those stances have been softened with the addition of job-induced mental anguish as a reason for such an act. Now, in my Peer Support role, I always offer the families full honors, always. It's become a regulatory thing now, anyway, that it should be done. Almost everyone wants the flag, and everyone deserves it.

After the funeral, my family stayed together. We had Joe's house to clean out, all the things to take care of that make up a life. Painful things. The members of his agency told us that they, too, were family, but they did not stick by us, only a few of his closest friends stood by my family. It was a bad, sad vibe. I told my little brother Mike that this stigma was probably going to spread to us, too. He only had five years in, I had ten years in; it was a weird, uneasy feeling, and it's hard to describe exactly. We knew our brother's death would set us apart, and we would be treated as though we were suicidal, too, or at least different, out of place, and had to be watched. It's just the way it was. They wouldn't watch us out of sympathy, they would watch us out of suspicion. We decided we had to get back to work; we had stayed for a couple of weeks and, even though the time had flown by, now we felt that, maybe, we had been gone a little too long.

My mom was so heartbroken, she wanted everything that Joe ever had, to remember him by. When my family went to Joe's house after his death, my Mom noticed several items missing from his home. Unfortunately and predictably, it turned into my task to try and solve the mystery of those items. The only way we could figure out to locate those belongings was to view photos taken on the day we lost Joe, to make sure they were in place at the time of his death. My brother Mike and I had to go to the Colonie Police Department, near Albany, to pick up his things, and later met with the investigator. I didn't want Mikey to see those images. "I'm demanding that you don't go in there," I told him, as big brothers do. He stayed out in the hallway. "I trust you," he said, and sat outside. No one wanted to see those images, no one. Especially not me. I'd seen it once and the memories, as I said, will stay with me forever. I wanted my little brother to remember his big brother the way he should, not the way I saw him for the last time.

The investigator pulled up the pictures taken at the suicide scene and clicked through them in front of me. I just remember the mouse clicks, like an old-time picture show, clicking, closeups of my brother, dead, on the floor of his own house, clicking. I tried to stay calm, and focused on the mouse clicks. Mouse clicks. I was writing things down, trying to hold back the tears. It was awful. I made notes of the items my Mom was looking for and couldn't wait to get out of that office.

As I sat in front of the investigator's desk and he flipped through photos that even the most callous of individuals would cringe at, I knew I would never forgive the people who had caused this tragedy. I just kept thinking of the insensitive, self-absorbed, self-righteous officers whose actions led directly to Joe's suicide. Joe experienced the ultimate betrayal. His own people had betrayed him, reported him for something they all did, treated him so that he knew he was no longer welcome. He paid them back with the ultimate sacrifice. They were shocked, but were still unable to admit wrongdoing. Impulsive or not, suicide is a finality and it makes a very impactful statement.

There was something else bothering me, too, and making me even more apprehensive about the organizations we worked for. Just prior to Joe's suicide, I want to reiterate that he could not and did not trust a soul in his agency. He and I had talked about getting an attorney and suing the New York State Police for inappropriate discipline. I have known others who, in similar situations, felt they had no other course of action available to them. We had put together notes and had a whole manilla envelope full of information in regard to that potential action. When I went back into the house after his suicide, they had tossed his house! The whole place looked like someone had broken into it, like someone was frantically looking for something; his bed mattress was flipped over, his dresser drawers were dumped out and the entire place had been thoroughly gone through. It was crazy and we never did find that manilla envelope.

I have had many people ask me if the culture has improved within the New York State Police. I truly have no idea how they now handle things inside. As I mentioned, some of their own employees have felt compelled to sue the State Police in regard to some questionable disciplinary decisions, and that can occur in many different situations. Some lawsuits have been successful and some have not. I do believe that they are getting better; I want to believe they are getting better. In January of this year, 2023, after a change of command, I was contacted to sit down with their Peer Support Officers, and was delighted to. Finally, after thirteen years of doing what I'm doing, all agencies are working together on the same sheet of music. That speaks volumes, it's a symphony. We are unveiling this culture and changing it, person by person, case by case.

Let's be clear on this. I don't hate the New York State Police. Their administration may believe that I hate them; they were certainly on the defense about Joe. They were defensive because what they did resulted directly in the death of one of their own and because I pointed out the truth of the matter. As the years have gone by, the organization has become more human and many have retired. I have never hated the NYSP as an entity. The only people I hate and hold accountable are the people who specifically contributed to Joey's death. They should be held accountable, and if they aren't in this life, I firmly believe they will get what they deserve in the afterlife.

MY OWN DOWNWARD SPIRAL

At this point I should give you the balance of my own background. After Joe got my academy appointment in 1996 I went through the Chautauqua County Sheriff's Academy, attended and graduated the Jamestown Academy in Western New York in 1997. I went back up to the 'North Country', far upstate New York, and worked with the Essex County Sheriff undercover for a few months before returning to school. I then found myself with the Ticonderoga Police Department in 2000, and transferred to Washington County Sheriff's office in 2003. In 2014 I became a patrol officer for the Sheriff's Office in Warren County which is where I will be through February of 2024. At that time, I am pleased to say I will retire to work full time with law enforcement and first responders in need of support. These departments are mostly rural counties in Upstate New York close to the Albany area.

After we lost Joe I returned to work, thinking, as I said, knowing, really, that I would be ostracized. There was no peer support there, nothing, and I didn't expect any, wasn't sure I needed any. My first day back was April 20th, 2008, which, especially before it was legal, was a day to celebrate marijuana and all that may entail. It's another day fifteen years ago that I can remember it like it was yesterday. Some days I can't believe it's been that long, and then I look in the mirror at my receding hairline and miss my brother, as I do every day, and it feels like he's been gone forever.

My shift was 9pm-7am; I was on my own until eleven and then we doubled up, that was the rule, for safety. I felt tainted in my uniform; it just didn't feel right. I was doing anything I could to stay busy those first two hours and not get on the road in the patrol car.

I finally got my shit together and was back in the saddle, driving, when we got the call for a potentially fatal car crash. My partner and I rolled up and saw an absolutely destroyed Cadillac and a hellacious scene; we found out later that the car had been 'borrowed' from someone's grandfather. There were three males and two females joyriding at a place called Putnam Flats, where kids and idiots go to drive fast and show off. They didn't slow down enough at the end and failed to navigate the corner.

The entire scene was carnage, absolute carnage. There was a little blonde girl wrapped around a tree, no exaggeration. We loaded her into the ambulance and she died on the way to the hospital. That girl was close in age to my daughter, and had gone to school with her. The other female had been thrown quite some distance and when we found her, she, too, was dead. The driver had to be hospitalized, and my partner went along because we needed blood samples, tests from him, to go through the processing and formal charges. When the ambulances left, everyone else was en route and I was on scene by myself waiting for the accident reconstruction unit to arrive. I felt my right hand start to tremble uncontrollably. My legs were weak and I was just shaking. I made my way back to my patrol car and grabbed my spare jacket, thinking I was going to get fired for certain. I recognized it as shock. I was checking myself and wondering if they were going to know I was crazy; I'd be out of work; I wouldn't be able to support my family. My mind was going a mile a minute, and I knew, because I lived the culture, that I couldn't tell anyone, couldn't afford the stigma.

By the time the first investigator arrived at the accident, I was back in 'Cop Mode', and did what I had to do, stayed on scene until dawn. I never told anyone what happened to me that night, and went home like nothing had happened at all. Things definitely weren't the same for me, and it was more than just the loss of my brother. I knew there was something very wrong. It was ten years of sights like I just described to you. Ten years of standing tall and strong when a real human being would cry, should cry. I had lost

Joe and I lost all my other support over the next eighteen months. I pushed them all away, and the relationship with my immediate family was incredibly strained.

After the accident on my first night back, it seemed like the fatalities were just piling up around me. There was a 911 call, a guy saying he was going to kill his wife and himself. I was the closest car, first on the scene. He obviously had a plan as well as an elevated location; he had even cut trees down across his driveway so no one could get close. We call this an 'active shooter', which is always tremendously scary and good for an adrenaline dump. I left my car on the road and was making my way to the house through the woods, all alone. I knew I had backup on the way, but my heart was pounding, my weapon drawn.

The house was an A-frame style, I could discern people on the basement level. The door was hanging open and I was yelling commands to them. The man was still on the phone, probably with dispatch, and I could see a television on in the background. I could also see a naked woman gasping for air; I didn't know if he had shot her already or what, and I was just screaming my protocol commands. I saw the guy rocking back and forth while he's watching TV; he did not respond to me at all. Finally, he looked right at me, put a gun under his chin and pulled the trigger in the beam of my high-powered flashlight. I specifically remember putting that .38 Special revolver into an evidence bag and walking out of the house saying to God, "Are you fucking kidding me, can I tap out? When is it going to stop? How much shit do I need to go through?" I even looked up at the sky, trying to see if he was up there, and I didn't see a damn thing. There were other horrific things that year, 2008, too many to count. Life was sad, perplexing, depressing and stifling. I trudged on, unable to move forward.

That year, and the year after, I always had a few drinks to get to sleep, and my habit, my need, got worse and worse. The problem was, if I didn't drink enough, I would have this recurring nightmare.

I would wake up startled and angry, incredibly angry at the injustice of it all. The nightmare was always the same, about the clicking mouse, that investigator flashing the last pictures ever taken of my brother across his screen. Clicking, clicking.

All the shit that was stacking up on me falls into the general category of trauma. That's what LE calls it. The Police1.com website defines trauma as: *"an event or circumstance that results in physical, emotional and/or life-threatening harm. It can have lasting adverse effects on the individual's mental, physical and emotional health and social and/or spiritual well-being.*

Trauma is prevalent within the law enforcement community, especially for those injured on the job. Police officers experience trauma in three ways:

* Acute trauma is a major traumatic experience such as a shooting that cuts through the survivor's mental "armor," overloading their system and leaving them feeling unprotected and dealing with more than they can handle.
* Layered trauma is the smaller, cumulative experiences that change an officer slowly. The figurative mental armor falls off over time – first an arm plate, then a leg piece – and after a few years there is no more armor left and seemingly no resources available to help the officer cope. The officer is essentially stripped of their ability to apply healthy coping skills in this type of scenario.
* Vicarious trauma is experiencing someone else's trauma after hearing or relating to their stories of traumatic experiences.

There's also a fourth category that significantly affects law enforcement: unresolved trauma. Unresolved trauma is complex trauma that has built up over time and has not been dealt with. For example, we've seen the effects of trauma in an officer who grew up in an abusive household and is then confronted with a call for abused children. The effect of that experience may force unresolved trauma to the surface.

The hyperarousal, re-experiencing and avoidance symptoms of trauma can make completing the most mundane tasks seemingly impossible. In many cases, those battling post-traumatic stress turn to drugs and/or alcohol as a means of coping. Unfortunately, self-medicating is like "saving the roof and shingles without dealing with the fire in the basement."

Furthermore, should the symptoms of post-traumatic stress remain present in an individual's life without alleviation, the anguish can worsen and trigger additional mental health concerns. Police officers experiencing trauma must do something to get the trauma out.

While most police officers go into law enforcement knowing they will be exposed to horrific scenes, many are not prepared for what can happen emotionally, psychologically and physically. Think of trauma as the proverbial death by 1,000 cuts: If untreated, it can result in emotional detachment, difficulty in relationships, depression, anger, complacency and, all too often, thoughts of suicide."

My work was obviously affected. I had been moved to a smaller substation within our county where there were less officers; that was the department's solution, to move me away. I was pissed off at everyone in the world, and had started to truly isolate. I did not want to be included; I didn't feel right. Much later, I learned, and now I understand, how common that is with what LE endures.

I didn't treat others as I used to treat them. I was on edge, upset, I just didn't care what was going on with anyone else. I wasn't myself, wasn't joking or laughing; I used to be the life of the party and I did a complete one-eighty. I didn't care about my appearance, my performance, or my demeanor. Just putting my uniform on was tough. Over the next year, 2009, there were more traumatic incidents than I can remember; I did what needed to be done but I didn't give a shit. I got a paycheck, that's the only reason why I went. My superiors knew it. My fellow officers knew it. *And still, no one ever asked me if I needed help*. No one. I got deeper and deeper into depression, pushed everyone away, even my wife. My condition took a tremendous toll on my family; I stopped doing things with my kids, no community activities, no coaching sports, I didn't deal with anything. It was absolute hell.

I'm not very emotional anyway, I had learned that from my dad, and now I was the King of keeping things bottled up. LE doesn't react like the general public because we see so much shit. I had one girlfriend tell me, "You're the coldest person I've ever known in my life." If you've ever met me, you'd know that is far from the truth. When something happens I don't get upset, I believe that everything can and should be taken in stride; that's an essential part of our LE training. It comes very naturally now, twenty-four years in the making. However, my emotions, during this period of my life, I simply could not take in stride.

It was a shock to me that I was someone who had developed into an asshole with a drinking problem. I had become one of those people I had learned to hate, and most importantly, I didn't have the energy or the focus to even care. I thought about every aspect of my life, the kids, my parents, and I still felt so alone. I had relied so much on Joey; I was trying to survive in the world without him and it wasn't easy. We used to talk about everything, and that luster, that outlet, was gone from my life; he had been my therapist, my sounding board, but I hadn't realized how important that was. I could vent, I could ask advice, whatever I needed. Joe had been my go-to. Most people don't have that. When it's gone it's gone and the healing will never be complete. It took me two years to find a different outlet, two years of self-destruction. I have learned enough self-awareness to know how I affect people and fortunately I got rid of the asshole a long time ago.

I also didn't believe in psychology. I truly didn't. And there wasn't a good resource I could utilize anyway, at that time. While I was not physically alone, I was mentally alone. By choice. I didn't know who I was, no one did. Was there something I could do? It was like I was on fire and they couldn't touch me, wouldn't touch me. I was on this island and didn't have anyone to look to. I was letting my family down; I was letting everybody down. I should have done more but I had no idea what to do, I honestly didn't. Like me and psychology, my family didn't 'do' mental health; it wasn't a common practice and I would say it was even looked down upon, thought of as a weakness. We were raised to be strong, and to manage whatever was thrown at us. I couldn't talk to them; Joey was gone and I had nowhere else to go.

In January of 2010, I found myself with my service weapon in one hand, and a bottle of booze in the other. I didn't want to die, but there was so much pain, I was suffering so badly every day that I didn't want to get up the next morning. It was a loop of constant distress and suffering, alone. While I was sitting there, contemplating my own suicide, I had this awful fleeting moment, and I heard my mom crying; she was at my funeral. I said to myself, "I need to do better, I cannot go on like this." I put my gun back in the dresser drawer and I picked up the phone and told the man on the other end not to call the cops, that if he did it would be over before they even got to my front door. "I don't want to die," I told him. "I just need help."

I AM NOT ALONE

That phone call was to someone I had met after my brother's suicide, an Employee Assistance Program (EAP) guy in some distant department who was a cop, and I told him in no uncertain terms that I needed to figure this out. Fortunately, he was able to make an appointment for me with a retired officer who had become a psychologist and worked specifically with law enforcement. Ironically, he was part of the same agency that Joe had been in, the State Police. I called in sick the next day, told absolutely no one that I was seeking help, and went to the appointment, two and a half hours away.

Today, as I write this, I cannot believe how afraid I was of the stigma, the backlash, the repercussions. I was terrified that they would take my guns away, that I would lose my job, lose my badge. I was petrified. I didn't know what psychology really was. I was terrified. Did I mention that I was terrified? It's worth repeating. The counselor and I just started talking; he brought me down and put me at ease. I went through a whole box of tissues, once I opened up about Joey, no kidding. I had locked all the traumas away. I was taught to suck it up and just move on. I didn't know that you couldn't, you shouldn't, just tuck those things away. I didn't realize that even though I was stuffing it all down that it was still in there and just waiting to show itself again. That hour went by in the blink of an eye.

I could see a tiny speck of light when I walked out of there. That tiny speck was the first time I had any sense of hope since Joey died. I continued seeing that counselor every week, and still told no one, especially not my Sheriff or anyone in the agency. After six months or so, and after trying to repair relationships and understand how I got to where I was, I felt better, lots better.

One of my colleagues asked me what was going on; he had noticed changes in me and my demeanor. I was suspicious immediately, and still afraid to admit I needed, and was getting, help. I told him I was okay but he kept hounding me, adamant about wanting to know what I was doing differently. So I decided, fuck it, I don't care anymore and I told him straight out I was seeing a therapist and that it had made a huge difference; I wasn't tearing my life apart anymore. I felt better, slept better, drank less, and understood much more about not only myself, but why I had changed so much. I remember standing there, at that moment, waiting for the ball-busting to start because that's what cops do. To my astonishment that officer simply asked, "Can I have his number?" Five little words. The skies parted, I saw the sunlight, it was amazing; *I wasn't alone.*

Even with that sunny revelation, I knew that most of my fellow officers were still afraid to talk about it. Afraid of the stigma. The very moment I shared the counselor's number I started helping other cops; that's how all of this began. I started gathering resources from everywhere I could think of, it was a grass-roots, organic thing. I was just trying to help, and I truly understood all about the confidentiality. Helping them was helping me. I knew this was a big deal, and that I could help more of us. Everything was done off-duty, none of it was paid for and none of it was publicly acknowledged at this point. I had found out very quickly that not only was I not alone, I had lots of company, all isolated from one another. Until now.

In 2013 I started teaching a class called TRAUMA with the New York State Division of Criminal Justice with some other instructors, and it was equally amazing. Here I saw further proof that training about suicide, substance abuse, health risks and mental health worked. It saved lives. I had many officers come up to me after those sessions and ask for help, and I was happy to assist. My mission was becoming more and more clear. We made it happen.

Around this time, 2014, I applied to work with the Warren County Sheriff's Office. In my interview I made it clear that I wanted to be able to continue working with those programs, I did most of it on my time off anyway. I was working seven days a week, but they knew what I was doing and they were supportive; it was a huge moment for me. I knew I was making a difference; I needed other people to know it, too.

"Banish is not getting paid for it, he's just making it happen," My Sergeant told the Sheriff a couple of years into my tenure at Warren County, and it must have made an impression. When I first started, the department, headed by Sheriff Nathan "Bud" York, helped me out a bit financially and gave me a gas card, a department car, permission, time, and an underlying authorization to help wherever I was needed. I was still working my night shifts and helping officers during the day; burning the candle at both ends, as the saying goes. About a year later, I had worked all night, and the next day was contacted about an officer from another department who was suicidal. I got an EZ pass from one of the sergeants so people knew I was going somewhere, and that I had to be back on shift at seven the next morning. At the time all of my work was, (and always will be), confidential, so it turns into a balancing act sometimes. I got home at four am and was scheduled to be in uniform at seven.

I walked in the door from that very stressful ride and a couple of hours sleep and was called to the Sergeant's office, where he told me that the Sheriff wanted to see me. This is a really big deal in the world of LE. I was absolutely scared to death, sweating, nervous, tired, wondering what the hell was going on. My Lieutenant walked me down to the big guy's office, so by then I was really sweating!

The whole rank and file for the agency came into the office; I could not believe it. I thought I was getting fired, the entirety of the brass in my agency was there. I don't have any brass, I'm just an officer. It was a very unusual situation; I remember every second of it.

"Jim," Sheriff York said, "There's a problem. You're getting called off the road more and more, and I'm worried about it. What I'm going to do is make this a full time position for you. If you think you can do this full time, let's do it and you can get some sleep in between." I was speechless, which is not a common thing. They didn't have anything planned or budgeted; they created the position just for me, that very day. I could see his intensity as he told me, "You're doing God's work and we want to support it." I was in tears, didn't know what to say or do, I was in such shock, and so proud. Peer Support Coordinator is my title; that Sheriff was old-school in many ways but he took a giant, progressive leap forward in taking care of law enforcement. I am incredibly grateful that he took that step. It made all the difference.

But. I wish there wasn't a 'but,' but in law enforcement culture there is so often an inherent fear of someone who is thinking differently, or acting differently, or reacting differently; it comes with a stigma, as we've talked about. The Peer Support Program, and my new role, regardless of the Sheriff's support, weren't truly welcomed in the department. I was treated the same as anyone else that had just gotten a promotion or special detail. Everyone talked behind my back and sometimes even disagreed with the program right to my face. In law enforcement, if you get something that other people don't, or do something that other people don't, even if they didn't want it or it had never existed before, somehow they hold it against you. I know that sounds crazy, but, again, it's part of the culture, this lack of generous human spirit. They thought it was ludicrous, weak, unnecessary, but I knew what I was accomplishing. I walked in every morning with a smile on my face that I maintained, despite their criticism. They didn't make it easy on me. I was weakening the foundation of their culture. I was saving and improving lives.

Hearts, souls, psychological armor. Those are the things LE doesn't teach. Just months after my appointment to Peer Support Coordinator, Sheriff York stated boldly, "Families and lives have been helped because of Jim already. He's a pioneer." Warren County was the first. The momentum was shifting. The "It's okay to not be okay" phrase was getting some attention.

Shortly thereafter, a member of my own agency became suicidal. He had spoken out against everything that I was doing, against the very creation of my position...and then I was tasked with helping him. It was a very ironic, slightly awkward situation. I honestly did not care what negativity he had caused, I got him through it. He lived and got to retirement, and we both know I helped him do that. After he had gotten treatment, we actually became close friends and we still are. His wife came to the sheriff's office, addressed the entire membership and told them they had no idea how much good I had done, that I had saved the officer and saved their entire family. Nobody had any idea because I kept it all confidential.

I had been working with this officer and his family for two years and nobody knew the insight and how deep my involvement really was. Things have shifted tremendously. This was a member of their own agency, one of their own. I saved this guy's life and I cannot tell you how much that means to me. No one was truly aware of what I was doing behind the scenes. That is the way it had to be. It used to be that if you showed weakness or independence, no one would talk to you. No one would trust you. That's just the way it was, and in a lot of places still is. In this culture, once you breach trust or confidentiality, or support the 'wrong' thing like Joe did, you're done. You might as well move on to something else because it won't be forgotten.

I knew then what I needed to change. And I am still going for it, full on, every day. Every day people join me. When I started to build this book in my head, I researched what other resources are out there. I think there are a couple good ones, some written by people who have been in the trenches, some not. What I found was that all of them teach you how to handle, how to manage, law enforcement culture *as it is*. None of them say, "Hey, let's save lives by *changing police culture*." It's not enough to manage it, we need to make it "Okay to not be okay." This book unveils the culture, and then gives those willing the permission to go forward with modifications that will make their life better.

I never want any other family to go through what my family went through. In my department, I was there when someone needed me, and I will continue to do that, regardless of their stance or opinion of what I'm doing. I take care of people, offer training and seminars, and travel all across the state and the country, although I still pull an occasional patrol shift. It's unfortunate that my mission requires a full time job, if you look at it that way, and we must. In fact, there should be many more positions just like mine, because the suicide numbers among LE are still rising. Thankfully, the trend is starting to change and more officers are being tasked with full time roles within their agencies. This is progress, big progress, and I'm only getting warmed up.

In June of 2017, there were three law enforcement suicides in NY alone, and #breakthestigma was created. A fourth individual credits me with saving his life. The weight of it all became so great that this particular officer wanted to die. I got to him, just in time. After what we see every day, you don't just say, "I'm all set." That's the truth.

Every time we save a life I call my mom and tell her we saved another one. I hope it helps ease her pain.

BLAME

As cops, we learn to keep our emotions secret, under control. That was what Joey wanted, and I had promised. Can you imagine how many times I've wondered if I had done or said something differently, would Joe would still be alive? It's a big fucking number.

My family was angry with me for not telling them about Joe's issues, about what he was going through. While I was fighting my own demons, I was alienated from them and everyone else. They felt that if I had told them, maybe the ending would have been different. That was what we had always done, shared our burdens, but only amongst ourselves. We did not show weakness or emotion to the outside world. To this day, the only time I have ever known my father to cry was in secret the morning after his oldest son took his life.

My family blamed me, and although they didn't say it outright, I knew they held it against me, somehow, that Joe was no longer alive. It sounds odd, now. It was not an overt blame, it was not a conversation, it was simply understood. They felt it was my fault and I could have done more. I didn't feel as included, as comfortable, because of that. Our conversations were less frequent, and there was conflict when I started speaking out against certain things. My sister chastised me at one point for using my brother's name in Peer Support Trainings. Here I was, trying to break through to people and use my tragedy for other officers to see that it's okay to get help, and she crushed me, crushed my soul, rocked me, demoralized me. I have never made a dime on his name. I have actually lost money, spent thousands and thousands of my own personal dollars to get this program to fruition. I could not understand her perspective. The conflicts festered.

My sister was, and probably still is, angry at the injustice of it all. Of course my entire family had tremendous pain from the loss. Everyone has, and does, grieve differently, and we were a non-therapy family, so what I was doing conflicted with the norm. My methods were healthier, so she took her anger out on me and I understood that, and I'm ok with it. A journey through grief is unique, and can lead us down very different pathways. No two people will grieve the same way, even if they are grieving the exact same incident.

For me, telling my story was altruistic, cathartic; it was healing me even though I dealt with the event over and over. At the ten year anniversary of Joe's death in 2018, my family planned to get together, for a mass. For several months prior, I was anxious; I no longer knew how to talk to my family because of what had happened. My therapist and I put a plan in place, a confrontation. We worked through the fact that it was not my fault, that I was not to blame. I was going to gather them and have a question and answer, deal with it and close the chapter. I could no longer be blamed. I had accepted his death, and it was not my fault, I knew that. We all knew that.

I was so inspired, so ready to make it happen that I just dug right into that whole conversation as soon as we were together. I had driven all night from New York to South Carolina to be with them. I told them that this was the time to ask any questions regarding Joey's death and that after this, I would be closing the book on the blame. I explained everything that I was doing, the therapy, the people I was helping every day, the lives I had already saved. It was simple, many tears were shed, and of course I wish I had done it much sooner.

New Year's Eve, like Christmas, had been a family tradition, but we stopped when we lost Joey. That year the tradition was revived and I found my mom crying in the kitchen. I went over to her and asked why she was crying. She apologized to me, and told me that she knew it wasn't my fault. I gave her the biggest hug and we cried together. We lost nearly ten years, but everything has been on the up and up since. I wouldn't have been able to survive without them so of course they are forgiven. My mom instilled that strength in all of us. Since that conversation, things have been immensely better for everyone. For me, it was more proof that human issues need to be brought out into the open and not carried around, dragging you down.

WE USED TO BE HEREOS

We used to be heroes and it was respected, it was truly an honor, to be a member of the law enforcement community. It was something that kids dreamed about and good people strived to be. That is no longer true. Our relationship with the public is now adversarial. I believe many negative incidents that happen with law enforcement could have been avoided if the people involved had followed the directions of the officer(s). I understand that confrontation with authority is stressful for both parties, and in my experience a lot of people simply don't do as we ask them to do. That can quickly escalate to more stress, and unexpected, dangerous situations that could potentially have been avoided.

Ninety percent of our career is pure boredom and ten percent is pure terror. When people don't do what we ask them to do, bad things can happen, and much of the time it is the officer that is forced to make very difficult decisions. I can hardly describe to you how stressful that is; human beings and all of God's creatures have very strong self-preservation instincts. We are constantly trying to balance keeping the public safe and keeping ourselves safe. I have never met, and you will never meet, an officer that wakes up every morning and says, "Well, I hope I get to take someone's life today," or "I can't wait to arrest someone and ruin their life." That's not how it goes, that's not how it is. The tremendous majority of us are out there every day doing a job, upholding the law and keeping the peace, not condoning hatred or violence.

Law enforcement takes the cream of the crop of society. The proof of that is in all of the testing and requirements that are necessary just to get into the academy. Law enforcement and first responder careers begin with a psychological exam, an extensive physical fitness exam, and a written exam. Upon acceptance, you have to excel at the academy, which is generally a six month, very intensive program not unlike military basic training, only longer. You have to be on top of your game. All the entities know your baseline is good upon graduation. That is proof positive that it is the job, and the responsibilities thereof, that brings these good people down. The life expectancy of police officers is fifty-seven while the national life expectancy is seventy-eight. That's a hell of a difference. As officers we need to process the trauma and relieve the stress but the ingrained culture doesn't allow you to admit to your peers that you have these feelings or that you're even human. It's vicious.

In police work we would call that a clue, and it's a big clue. All of LE; *everyone* is affected in one way or another; suicide rates, physical disease leading to early death, divorce, isolation. Two hundred and forty-eight officers or retired officers took their own lives in 2019, according to Blue H.E.L.P., another non-profit organization that is trying to reduce the stigma tied to mental health treatment for LE. Our suicide rate is exponentially higher than average, it was never before paid attention to. Suicide rates weren't even tracked within law enforcement until just five years ago, until then, the government had not acknowledged the problem. According to CBS News in 2021, suicide takes three times more law enforcement lives annually than officers killed in the line of duty and it took a long time to have officer suicides classified as line of duty deaths. We as a nation must understand that it is the job, its culture and its responsibilities that kills those officers just the same as someone else's bullet. Thankfully, there was a bill passed by President Biden in 2019 which determined that if a suicide is related to the job, it is considered a line of duty death.

Here's one of my personal issues, pet peeve or whatever you want to call it; the government provides benefits in the case of an LE officer that has a heart attack. Wouldn't it be better if the government put their money into proactive programs such as our LEAP (Law Enforcement Assistance Program), to give officers the intellect and the mindfulness to prevent their own degradation? It's so fucked up. So backwards. We should fund the prevention and the wellness of our people, not give them money after they have suffered or lost their lives altogether. Statistically, the role of LE is more and more essential as our country becomes more violent, yet we have been forced to drop our standards drastically in order to recruit. All of the standards. College requirements, background check standards, even agility and physical requirements are less than they used to be. As you would expect, in return, you get a lower quality force, no longer quite the cream of the crop. Correctional officers can just apply online and get hired! It's that desperate.

Therefore, there is even less time to take a breather between incidents, meditate, recoup and relax. Your next call is already waiting for you before you even get done cleaning up your last fatal. This job is non-stop and we are feeling the pressure, even worse than before because every agency is short staffed and now mandatory overtime is in place to cover more shifts. This proud nation is over a hundred thousand officers short nationwide, and that number is continuing to grow. How can an officer have any down time or any time at all to process or be proactive?

Most civilians encounter, on average, six critical incidents in a *lifetime*. The last statistic on this I saw was that LE encounters at least one hundred and eighty-eight critical incidents in a twenty-year career. That's why we are meant to be a renewable resource to the community. We simply burn out from overexposure to trauma. We don't have time to debrief every call, and we don't take time to discuss and process how we're feeling after almost being killed. We have to finish our shift, complete our paperwork, and then respond to the next call, so we just tuck the traumas away. We store those emotions in a bucket, or put them up on a shelf for as long as that shelf will hold. Let me tell you from first-hand experience, that bucket will eventually fill up and spill over, and that shelf is bound to break at some point. When it does that officer will have to deal with it because it's not going away on its own.

We were heroes and now we're zeros. Television, media and social media is demonizing law enforcement, all organizations, hands down. Presidents have shredded us. "Defund the police," protestors said, burning our cars and endangering our lives. Our own people are demonstrating against us, and promoting violence toward us! Similar to Joe's situation, it is the ultimate betrayal, not to have the support of the very people we are sworn to 'Protect and Serve.'

Now it's gotten to the point where we are so incredibly scrutinized it's hard to do our job. Imagine this; you're monitored even on the way to work by your car-mounted camera. Then we wear body cams (Body-Worn Cameras, or BWCs); which are becoming more and more mandated by departments nationwide. BWCs record every conversation on a call, all day long, every word, every moment. At the time of this writing seven states mandated use of body cams on all officers and thirty-four states were considering similar legislation, according to *World Population Review*. The fact that we are being so closely monitored is discouraging and demoralizing in itself; it means that the people we work for don't trust us, the public doesn't trust us.

The body cam issue is multi-faceted and has allowed us to realize how many officers, every day, day in and day out, do an outstanding job. Many smaller departments instituted BWCs and have since ended the programs because of the cost of data storage. They were learning what they already knew; that most cops do a damn good job; they follow the rules, they help people and they save lives. The transparency is fine. Both we and the public must remember it is the very minute minority of LE that behave badly and are subsequently made famous by the media. The rest of us started out working hard, loving our jobs and upholding our oaths only to be criticized and bastardized to the point where we don't want to even go out in public. Worse yet, politics get involved and we turn on each other.

Some people who aren't in the LE culture tell me the public no longer sees us as entities who protect and serve, but people who are to be feared and criticized. Many people feel that cops are just out to intimidate and get a revenue quota, even though the badge still says differently. I think that also reflects on how we see ourselves, which is much more negatively than we used to. So, in a vicious cycle, that's exactly what we do, we become wary of the public. We connect as little as possible. That is never how I saw my job; I always wanted to be the good guy, but I stopped feeling that way somewhere along the line. I know that now and it's so crazy. If I stayed busy and exhausted myself I didn't have time to think and that was better. Now, of course, after Joe, after years of service, I look at things completely differently.

When I was a rookie in 1996, there were no smartphones, no cameras and no video. Even though becoming a police officer was a huge reality check, I loved it. Fast forward to 2023 and everyone has a device close at hand that can record us at all times (in addition to our own). As LE we are under scrutiny non-stop. I call it hyper-vigilance; we cannot be human beings; we are not allowed to make mistakes. We work ten to twelve hour high-stress shifts, and then are expected to go home, forget it all, rest and recuperate. Alcoholism is rampant. Same with metabolic syndrome, which can encompass any or all of the following: high blood pressure, high blood sugar, excess fat around the waist, and abnormal cholesterol levels. Those issues lead to increased risk of heart disease, stroke and diabetes. There is a constant barrage of stress, administrative requirements, paperwork, the body cams, the videos, the pictures. Laws, too, have changed, so it's even more stressful than in the past. How much pressure can society continue to put us under? Why would anyone want to be a cop? Remember the life expectancy? Twenty years lower than average.

Let's talk about the concept of Bail Reform. In New York State, for most crimes, the accused won't go to jail, and there will be no bail set. Surprised? This was designed to decrease crowding in jails and to ensure that people unable to afford bail would not be unjustly and prejudicially incarcerated prior to being found guilty. Bail reform may be appropriate in some instances. However, because of this reform, in April of 2023 a man arrested on domestic charges in our jurisdiction was released twice. Twice. He went back, threatened his family for the third time and thank God we could then keep him detained. How does that affect his wife and children, when we cannot protect them even though they have called us over and over? How does it affect the officers that know it's not right to let that guy back out on the street? Some crazy things can happen, and more politics get involved. It is simply another way the hands of law enforcement have been manacled, and our effectiveness, both in reality and in the eyes of the public, diminishes through no fault of our own.

Why can LE retire after twenty years? Because mentally and physically very few individuals can perform well any longer than that. The problem is that we are losing many cops to retirement and we cannot replace them. We also have what we call 'retired on duty' people. They know exactly what the minimum is they need to do to keep their jobs and they do nothing more. The energy and the zeal to do the right thing is gone. They follow their leaders no matter what. They don't want to get involved with the shit, the politics, the drama, and they're just passing time. It's ineffective, inefficient and disheartening. Is it surprising to anyone that we have a tendency to self-destruct?

The clinical term for what I am describing is Cumulative Career Traumatic Stress (CCTS). As I mentioned briefly, I think of it as pebbles in a bucket; each incident is a pebble tossed in and it gets heavier and heavier, harder and harder to carry around, harder and harder to bear. Like the straw that broke the camel's back, it can be a small incident that all of the sudden makes the job simply too much to process, too much to manage on your own. A fellow officer and friend dying early in my career was the first trauma that put not a pebble but a stone into my bucket. Some traumas are like that. Trooper Larry Gleason died during what should have been a routine domestic call on February 11, 2002; that's how I really learned about my own mortality. One minute he was there and the next he was gone. In my case, the stone that overflowed my bucket was the death of Joe, but I didn't understand that at the time, and the pebbles just kept coming.

I completely understand why no one wants to do this job anymore. When I enrolled at the academy I thought it was going to be the best twenty years of my life. The current conditions reduce us down to just wanting it to be over, even me. I'm looking forward to my retirement, I can promise you that. We are seen as a replaceable/renewable resource. But high quality people are not coming on board. We don't want people to join us just for the benefits! We want, and need, people like Joe who were passionate and dedicated. We need to show them that if they take care of themselves that this can be a rewarding career and then ultimately enjoy their retirement for much longer than age fifty-seven. It's all about emptying that bucket and staying on top of your own wellness.

In a twist of fate I had not foreseen, my oldest son Domanic decided to join law enforcement. I told you he was the spitting image of my brother Joe, acted like him, looked like him, even thought like him, apparently. I imagine you can predict my response. Here's the story.

Domanic was an amazing athlete in high school; he received many offers to compete at the collegiate level, chose none of them and entered Army basic training at seventeen. He had decided on the Army Reserves, went to his Advanced Individual Training (AIT), and shortly thereafter he was deployed overseas for eighteen months. When he returned, his duty done, we had a conversation I will never forget.

"We need to figure out your future," I said to him, "What are you gonna do?" "Dad, I want to be a cop," he told me. "You're fucking crazy," I said, just like that. "Don't do it." He wanted to follow Joey, and then become a canine officer. I was surprised and not surprised, if that makes any sense. In the end, of course, I supported him, but set him up to not be accepted in New York because he was not yet twenty-one yet. Also, honestly, I wanted him to make his own mark and not be known as Jim Banish's kid.

Determined, he headed to my brother's place in Virginia, passed the tests and immediately they started his background investigation. He was accepted but still had to wait for the next class because he still wasn't of age. Although it makes me proud, I know what he's in for. He flew through their academy and became a Trooper. Like most law enforcement, Virginia has a six month training program; people at the top of the class get requests fulfilled, but they send you wherever they need you. That's the way it has to be. It turned out that Joey's badge number was available and my brother arranged to have it given to Domanic. It was an amazing moment, carrying on the family traditions. I went down and was honored to do the badge pinning ceremony, handed him his diploma at his graduation ceremony, me in uniform, him in uniform. It *was* truly amazing, but again, I knew, I know, what he is in for and I don't wish it on him. He's probably part of the reason I am so driven to change this culture and make law enforcement a more rewarding, healthier line of work. He's in the honeymoon phase, around five years in, and has already been promoted to canine officer. He has his dream job with a Dutch Shepard named Abza. He has done remarkably well; I think a lot of it has to do with his upbringing; he gets the culture. It was something he wanted to do and he went for it, all in, just like his Uncle Joe.

You know what else? Domanic has a hell of a head on his shoulders and is aware of the dangers, both physical and mental. He loves his job, taking drugs off the street. I call him the Kilo Kid because he keeps making it happen. I'm not just proud, I'm incredibly proud. You know what I'm most proud of? That he knows he can reach out for help if he ever needs it and that he will be able to perceive his fellow officers reaching out. Domanic was in just a couple of years and he understood people already, the human side. There was an incident, an infant death, to which an officer had a tremendous adverse reaction. I believe infant death calls are the hardest, especially when you have children of your own. My son called and asked me what to do, and then he utilized those resources, probably saving that guy's career. Domanic recognized the symptoms and helped him out, still in private, still confidentially, because there remains the stigma, this stigma that we are desperately trying to decrease, to erase, even, if we can. I never taught Dom the role of peer support officially, but he grew up in a house where his dad was always taking care of other officers, so that must have rubbed off a little. Or a lot.

Domanic and his fellow Troopers responded to the bullshit at the capital in Washington DC on January 6, 2022, the 'Insurrection.' My family watched that on television, fearing for everyone. And that same year I remember one night my phone rang, late, and he said "Dad, my will is in the safe and all the instructions are in there. I'm headed to an active shooter call," and then he hung up. I had to stress out until I heard from him again. This is the life we lead. There was an officer shot and killed that night; the times like that are too numerous to mention. And yes, I get scared. I worry. I'm also honored, thrilled, that he's following Joey's path, being the best he can be, and I'm sure Joey is, too.

www.NYLEAP.org

66

LAW ENFORCEMENT CULTURE

Let's talk about the power of the position, the power of a law enforcement officer. In the academies, they teach you that you are always in control. It is instilled upon you, that you have the power to make things turn out well. This is how they set you up for failure, honestly. We all recognize that there are many things in life that human beings cannot control, and included in that list is the next perpetrator that you encounter. Then, when shit does happen, the average fellow officer just says, "Suck it up Buttercup. You're a cop. Deal with it. You made your choice." That was, and in many places still is, the culture. It's a weird anomaly. The control you thought you had turns into, "Oh well, better luck next time. Move on. You'll be okay."

I have the opportunity to teach at many police academies all over New York State and that is a responsibility I take very seriously. I like to give cadets the realities of the path they have chosen, the responsibility to fairly enforce and uphold the law. I give it to them straight without bullshit or sugar coating. I want them to know what to expect from this career and how to prepare them for it, not only physically but psychologically. Once I discovered the mortality rate of law enforcement, and all of the health issues that go along with this career, it always perplexed me that we don't prepare our officers for that aspect of their lives.

As I've emphasized, we try to take the best that society has to offer when hiring law enforcement officers. Even though we have been forced to lower standards, a candidate still needs to pass a psychological test, vision test, physical agility test, and a written exam, just to be considered. Then there is a background investigation. That's all before you are selected for the academy, so if you look at the baseline of a new officer, it shows that they are mentally and physically fit, with high morals. That being said, law enforcement should be outliving the rest of the population. Why is it then that we are developing all of the health issues, and killing ourselves at such a high rate? It just doesn't add up. The most important thing here that wasn't previously factored in, is all of the trauma an officer has to deal with over twenty-plus years.

When I'm doing an Inservice Training anywhere in the country, I ask "Are you the same person today that you were before you started this career? Do you look at the world the same way? Do you treat people the same way?" The answer is always no and it's usually emphatic. I can pick out cops anywhere. We are hyper-vigilant and cynical, very aware of our surroundings; it's difficult to go to venues like concerts where there are crowds. It may sound crazy but we just aren't comfortable in a lot of places where other people go to relax and enjoy themselves. We don't like people; we don't like to be around them. It's not normal; we don't think or act normally. This job changes you; it changes how you see the world; it changes how you act in public; it determines where you sit in a restaurant, and many other idiosyncrasies. We do this because it's how we survive. We are constantly scanning for danger, 'carrying' off duty just in case, ready to jump into action at any given moment.

I use the term hyper-vigilant because we cannot turn it off at the end of our shift. It's not inherited. It's learned survival. We use dark humor and coping mechanisms like alcohol to wind down, to sleep, to help us forget the trauma that we have seen. We isolate and self-medicate; all of the horror and fear we experience bottles up and adds up. That level of vigilance is very difficult to maintain. It may be the reason why we are so cynical, have so much hate, and don't like to be around people. We are often dealing with the worst that society has to offer, and we get to a point where we see almost everyone as bad and question every good intentioned person out there, so how could we expect anything different? So, I ask you, the officer reading this book, "Are you the same person today that you were before this career?" If you can't recognize yourself in the mirror, then don't expect anyone else to. For those members of the public, can you see the changes in the law enforcement officers you know? Think about it. This job is our identity, the badge is who we are. I am Officer Banish, that's who I am. My brother panicked, took his life, at the thought of losing his badge, his status, his identity, his pride in all that he had accomplished. If you do this job long enough that identity takes over, and it doesn't take all that long.

I am as honest as the day is long, I get that from my Mom. It's gotten me into a lot of trouble and it's done a lot of good. Now, if I see something wrong, I walk into the Sheriff's office, tell him, and then say, "Have a nice day." I'm not keeping any of this stuff in anymore. Keeping it in almost killed me. If I see something wrong I'm going to say something. I've seen what happens when people don't. Firsthand. Since 2010 I've been speaking and teaching all over the country. When I do events such as Post Critical Incident Seminars (more on that later) I call it the light bulb effect. It's the same everywhere and it's what happened to me, the tiny light at the end of the tunnel that gets bigger if you do things right. We're all dealing with the same shit and when we feel like we're not alone it saves lives, marriages, health and happiness. Often times people will come up to me when I'm done speaking and say things like, "Oh my God, it was like I was checking off all the boxes as you spoke; that's me, too." The reality is that it's all of us. The silence has been broken and it's okay to talk about the shit we do and see, and better yet, to have normal reactions to an abnormal amount of bullshit. That's what these jobs really are, an abnormal amount of bullshit mixed in with moments when we truly are the hero.

I'm generalizing here, but I also feel safe in saying that career law enforcement officers feel like everyone could potentially cause them harm and everything is bad. Let me tell you firsthand, it's very hard having such a negative perspective on the world. The first five years of the career I call the honeymoon phase. The 'Dirty Harry' phase, when it's great to be a cop. You have a weapon, you have prestige, you are an achiever. You are the *Thin Blue Line*, stopping the world from chaos, doing the right thing. You are the good guy. When I was five years in, I still wanted to be part of that. I so loved belonging that I would work for free! I loved it just like my son does now, five years in.

Years five to ten the critical incidents start to add up; you have seen so much bad shit that it's hard to remember the good people and that people can be good. You don't sleep as well at night and you drink too much during your days off or engage in unhealthy acts. There are repercussions; you start to back your truck into the driveway for safety, you start to pull away or avoid situations and people you used to be able to enjoy. As time goes on, it's not necessarily your fault, and you start to get a bit jaded. You don't want to, but gradually, you do. You stay in because you're not sure what else to do. You begin to isolate, or just hang with a few fellow officers who have the same perspectives you do. In most cases, the same negativity. The atmosphere surrounding much of law enforcement is inherently caustic.

Years ten to fifteen into your career you start asking yourself why you're here, why you're doing what you're doing, with so little appreciation. You reach the cynical stage. You begin to hate the world, people, the news---oh, the news media, as I mentioned before, can shed such a bad light on LE that you want nothing to do with it, or them. Everybody on the force starts their 'countdown clocks'; sometimes as far as ten years from retirement! It's just the benefits they want, it's not to protect and serve like it used to be, and as I said, most are not sure what else they would do. There are too many politics and too much bullshit and incredibly, the negativity just gets worse and worse.

It's tough when you get attacked physically or mentally. We are trained to de-escalate, stay in control and move on. We swore an oath to protect the public. We're not allowed to do illegal things. The officers who react badly often have way too many pebbles in their bucket. They need to undergo the programs and/or therapies that we are talking about here. They have a very short fuse; most of those harmful incidents occur late in their careers. Let's talk about

George Floyd, a name we unfortunately all recognize. That officer (and I am not defending the result of his actions), had probably dealt with a similar individual hundreds of times without emptying his bucket. When all we see are assholes, we forget that we took this job to help people, to save them from themselves sometimes. The more shit we deal with, the more likely we are to use excessive force to protect ourselves. The public sees this as us taking it out on the public. Under more pressure and scrutiny than ever, can you blame those officers for reacting defensively? And since the public doesn't understand these pressures, can you blame them for being shocked when perpetrators die in custody? It's shocking to law enforcement, too, I assure you. It's all bad. For everyone. What I would guess happened in the George Floyd case is that his fellow officers abandoned him and ostracized him instead of supporting him, somewhere along the line. I don't know that for a fact, but I've seen similar situations where people were hung out to dry.

I see it most often when an officer gets investigated or disciplined on the job. His/her peers turn away from them instead of supporting them in a time of need. This is especially scary because now that officer feels alone. Take it from me, alone is not a place you want to be or feel. It's like you have the plague when you get jammed up. Nobody wants to be seen talking to you or with you, nobody even wants to shoot the shit at the station with you. They all feel like they might get roped into whatever is going on with you or that administration may look down on them for even affiliating with you during this time of investigation or discipline. In my opinion it's backwards, it's a contradiction.

LE officers simply don't live the same way as the general public. That's the culture. It's a caustic culture. I can't even describe it in one word. Unfortunately betrayal comes to mind. There is so much betrayal. You go in thinking everyone will have your back, but they don't. They'll fuck you over. We all get along and then someone gets promoted, they get the stripes, or get reprimanded, whatever, really, that makes them different. Then, their previous 'friends' are talking behind their back, talking shit. They just do that to make themselves feel better; it's a bad deal. We are supposed to be brothers, but we can't be happy for each other. These men and women who say you're their brother will turn and run in an instant when times get tough for you. These are the times where you need some help and insight, and quite possibly some support, from your own people. When their colleagues are struggling, unfortunately, LE tends to back away, just when their people need them the most. Oh, and here's the norm; no one will say anything bad to your face, but many will judge you silently behind your back. It's a very private culture and we like to handle things ourselves. It's ironic; I isolated myself but didn't really want to be alone. No one wants to get involved with shit. In my story, after Joe died, no one knew what to do or what to say. So in my case, no one said anything; they left me completely alone and that sure as hell didn't work.

Here's the surprise. On the complete opposite hand, working in law enforcement can be great, and very rewarding. Let's clarify this. LE *can* be an amazing family, and they *can* be a tremendous support. It is by nature a protective brotherhood, it is a culture, a career, where you have another's life in your hands. Literally. Whether you like that person or not, they have your life in their hands too. Everything about this job is our identity; the uniform, the gun, and the badge; you are identified as an officer. It quickly becomes who we are; we belong to something. This is the positive side of the culture, when things are good. For example, funerals truly demonstrate the brotherhood; lines and lines of officers in uniform honoring the fallen. After Larry's death I got close to his crew and have developed tremendous bonds with people elsewhere, too, some wonderful people. We feel that we cannot rely on other members of our society so we lean on each other. Until we can't. There's that contradiction again.

We need to be better. I make it a point to reach out to anyone who gets jammed up so they know they aren't alone. If I am made aware, I'll be there for them no matter what. That's how I train my peers, that's how we should all be trained from the very beginning of our careers. Whether the officer was right or wrong in any situation, it shouldn't cost them their life or their career. Let's be real, what does it cost you to reach out and check on someone going through a very difficult time? From my perspective, it could be the difference between life and death. I would never condone wrong behavior or excessive force; I'm trying to prevent those mistakes with education and wellness from within before the situation rises to that level. We need to work together to empty our buckets before they are too full. The negativity is contagious and deadly.

After all this, you then retire, and are separated from your people, your society, your brotherhood. There is a tremendous transition that needs to be prepared for. The brotherhood is so tightly knit that we see a tremendous number of suicides in retired cops as well as those still in uniform. Officers need to work their way out of the culture and into civilian life, they need to empty that bucket. It's hard for us to imagine that the job will go on without us, that we won't be missed and there won't be a huge parade when we leave or a day of honor to remember us, because in our mind we have given this job everything. All of the holidays, birthdays, special events away from the family. We do it because it's what we are supposed to do, and we accepted that when we took this job. That doesn't make it any easier when you walk out the door and don't have the comradery that you have grown accustomed to. It's like a water valve that gets shut off, one minute you have this Blue Family, the next you have RET after your name. It's just not the same, and it doesn't take long for people to forget about you.

What you can do is prepare for this transition by emptying your bucket. Go to a therapist, start enjoying your hobbies, start interacting with civilians. I always say that this should start with around five years left on the job. Find your purpose again, discover something new and engross yourself in it. Start to get out of that law enforcement mindset, that everyone is bad and has a hidden agenda. This takes a very conscious effort because it's the exact opposite of what you've been doing your entire career. I can assure you that you are replaceable; everyone is. The day after you retire there will probably be someone else's ass in your seat. It's meant to be that way, it's not personal. We are meant to be a renewable resource, but finding fresh troops has proven more and more difficult for all the reasons I am describing to you. Our society needs to understand that the human mind is not meant to see what we see and do what we do for such a sustained period of time and that's why we get to retire in twenty or twenty-five years. We *deserve* to retire in that timeframe! There aren't any towns like Mayberry out there anymore, and our society gets more and more complicated.

Almost everybody has that countdown clock, to leave the job behind, and then ironically many come back and work part time, to be part of something again. It's another anomaly, another contradiction. Humanity likes to belong. Normally an officer will spend more time at work than at home. The blue family vs. the blood family. They have plans to do all these things in retirement, instead they often become sedentary. And then, what we are seeing and starting to understand is that the trauma can really come back, even after all those years, if they never got rid of their buckets of pebbles and stones and memories.

Handling the aftermath of what we do was never talked about, the psychological armor that I mentioned was not part of our training. That's why I started teaching in the academies, and that's why Joe did, too. It allows me to influence recruits at the beginning as well as after the traumas are experienced. I tell them that it's okay to react as a human being, to be out of control for a few minutes, and then you should, you must, come back to your level of homeostasis. We were never allowed to talk about this stuff before. LE sees more trauma in six months than a normal person experiences in an entire lifetime. We don't have a job that affords us the time to process most things that have happened, we have another call to go on, someone else needs help, so we just put it in the bucket for another day. For twenty years we do this with no warning of what we will have to manage next! Twenty years. Give us a fucking break already.

We deal with everyone else's shit as well as our own. The worst for most of us, like with the officer in Virginia, is infant mortality and child abuse. Children getting hurt seems to be what really creates long term traumas and reinforces that the world is not a good place. Those calls put more and more pebbles into buckets. Let me reiterate, working a beat is ninety percent boredom and ten percent sheer terror, or chaos, or both. Some days the stress is indescribable. We never know what we're going to walk into; every single day is different. We have to be ticket writer, social worker, police, medic, and mental health evaluator. In one twelve hour shift, you can get a high-five from some little kid, which is great, and then there can be a shooting, and then it's some easy little traffic stop. You're a chameleon and you're expected to perform perfectly. You're on camera. That's a lot of hats to wear in one day. We ask you to do this for twenty years. We don't have a job that affords us the time to process most things that have happened. We have another call to go on, someone else needs help, so again we just put it on the shelf, in the bucket, for another day. At what point are there too many things on the shelf? Everyone has a different level of tolerance. We're also much the same.

As an officer, you create your routine. At first, during that honeymoon phase, you're compassionate, empathetic. Then you tend to develop a callousness that will eat you up because it's not human. The public doesn't expect us to be human and they think that we can handle anything. That's not fair. We are human. Remember Uvalde, the school shooting in Texas? The police got crushed by the news and the truth of it is they didn't engage because they were obeying orders. It was a mess and they were criticized for that, the interviews with those first responders afterwards told us that they wanted to go in and were not allowed to do so. Another strike against law enforcement which was made much worse by the media.

I admittedly have an issue with the media. These mass shooting perpetrators, they are going to be recognized for a long time, famous even. When Columbine happened in Colorado, the first major school shooting, everybody knew the two shooter's names, but not the kids who were murdered. The shooters will be known forever; part of their goal was immortalizing their own names. Do we know the names of the SWAT guys that got everybody else safely out of that situation? Do we know who those heroes are? The ones that had to see the bodies of the kids and teachers in the hallways and in the library? No, we do not.

I feel that the media outlets cover these atrocities in a way that they shouldn't. It's that simple and gives the bad guys exposure and fame. I support freedom of the press and freedom of speech, but these events pose a lot of complicated issues, the mental health laws, gun control laws, and when you get politics involved everything gets screwed up. I know that's a generalization and not really what this book is about, but I had to toss it out there.

Now, in eighteen states, individual citizens can call the police and have another person's rights removed. That's not how our forefather's wrote the Constitution. When one of these requests come in, we, as the designated officer, have to go in front of a judge and try to determine if it's the right thing to do. Tough decision, right? Red Flag Laws, as they are called, prevent individuals who show signs of being a threat to themselves or others from purchasing or possessing any kind of firearm. And maybe it's even a decent idea. But who enforces these politically motivated concepts? Law enforcement does. It's not an easy job. None of it is. There aren't a whole lot of folks in this country that will happily hand us their Second Amendment Rights, their weapons.

The symptoms of CCTS, Cumulative Career Traumatic Stress, are very similar to PTSD, Post-Traumatic Stress Disorder, which has become a common terminology in the last couple of decades, mostly connected with the military. It's known now and the public is sympathetic, but let me tell you there was little tolerance for the Vietnam Veterans that came home with it. They were different, they were ostracized, they couldn't function normally; they saw the world as a shitty place because of what they had seen and experienced. And, four or five decades ago, there was definitely no one to help them, either. Suicide rates skyrocketed. As a society, we must begin learning from history and allowing people to admit that they are not okay. That it's okay to not be okay. It's okay to need help. Asking for help is not weakness, it is strength.

I was, in fact, officially diagnosed with PTSD. I still have my gun and my badge. I never lost them. That diagnosis is not a negative thing; it was not and is not an inhibitor for my career or my life. If you end up with PTSD, there are ways to process those traumas and continue living a productive, successful life. I'm proud that I prevailed. I learned how to manage it; I am now teaching other people how to manage it. That's the crux. That's the goal. I'm not embarrassed by it, I'm proud of it. I'm proud that I've been able to live with my PTSD. As I told you, there was a time when I felt unable to live with it. I have something within me, something I cannot exactly identify, that kept me from ending up just like my brother. I think it was the desire to make a change in the world I had chosen, a desire to stop the spiral.

I know that I'm not perfect or perfectly recovered, and my PTSD can manifest. It will, and when it does, and I do something about it. I understand it, and I do something about it. I still see a clinician regularly, over a decade after I began. I keep a level of homeostasis, I dump the pebbles out of my bucket, and stay on an even keel. Here I am, a cop admitting that I'm in therapy. It was unheard of fifteen years ago because of the possible retributions, because LE used to follow the crowd. Someone could take your gun and your job. It was seen as a weak act, a sign of instability.

The headlines in this week's *Boston Globe* as I write this tell us that the members of the Boston Police Department that added overtime hours to their timecards when, in fact, they had not worked overtime, were acquitted. Clearly, what they did was wrong; it is illegal, it is stealing from the people of Massachusetts. It is fraud, it is deception. The members of that force were acquitted because "they were merely following longstanding practices accepted by department leadership... There is no dispute that they falsified documents and got paid for hours that they did not work." According to the Judge, what they did was not a crime, because *that's the way it's always been done.* Just because things have always been done a certain way doesn't mean it's the right way to do them. The culture of that entire department allows ongoing crimes to be committed by their own officers. That fraud is also now supported by the Judge in that case; it was determined they were innocent of wrongdoing *even though what they were doing was wrong.* That's fucked up. It's part of what I am trying to change, one person, one department at a time. Together we can change this culture.

Don't be a victim, don't follow the crowd. The world and your department doesn't owe you anything; it's on you to make your life the best it can be, and to take care of yourself along the way so that you can be the best version of yourself. Because of the path I chose, there will be events from my career that will stick with me for the rest of my life. I still would not have chosen differently.

Don't have the mindset that somebody owes you something, or you are entitled to a position or promotion or a special detail. If you find that a career in and commitment to law enforcement is not for you, it's okay to leave and go find another path. You have to ask yourself, is my life worth it and do I want to be a part of this negativity for the rest of my life, or do I want a better environment? Would I do the wrong thing like the boys in Boston just because everyone else was doing it? We all have the power to break the negative, caustic culture. There are so many good things that LE does and we need to start sharing the glory and being proud of who we are. We used to be heroes; we can be heroes again.

www.NYLEAP.org

LEAPING FORWARD

In my twenty-fourth year of service, I am very proud to call myself President and Founder of the New York Law Enforcement Assistance Program (NYLEAP) www.NYLEAP.org. NYLEAP is a two-fold program; we confidentially assist officers in need of support through Post Traumatic Incident Seminars (PCIS) and Peer Programs. The clinicians and therapists that work with me are peers and all have experience in law enforcement or the military; we refer to them as Culturally Competent Clinicians. Otherwise, the program would not work. It's important to stress the need for a culturally competent clinician. They are clinicians familiar with our culture; they have a family member in law enforcement, were at one point themselves officers, or they have been around the culture enough to know and understand why we are the way we are and why we talk the way we do. I believe if any standard clinician were to walk into a stationhouse locker room and hear the shit we say and how we talk about incidents, they would want to lock us all up. It's part of our culture, it's part of how we handle the constant negative atmosphere and the horrific calls we are constantly exposed to.

As I told you, when I was twenty, my brother Joe got me an appointment to the Police Academy and I am glad he did. As you also know, Warren County, New York, turned out to be one of the best moves I ever made. The then-Sheriff was visionary and allowed me to apply myself full-time to my passion, saving lives. I've taken guns out of cop's mouths more times than I can count at this point in my life, both literally and figuratively. That means that Joe's death was a tragedy that has led to something positive.

For me, Peer Support really began in 2010, when I contacted an Employee Assistance Program, started therapy, saw the light, and then found other resources on my own time. When I started teaching TRAUMA for the NY Department of Criminal Justice, that led me on to other programs, one of which was NYLEAP, which turned the path of my life again. Where Peer Support Programs have been established or made readily available, officers have an outlet and it works. Peer Support works. A lot of LE didn't (and still doesn't) get help because of this stigma that we keep coming back to. Who in the hell wanted to go to their superiors and tell them, admit to them, that they needed help? No one, not even me.

My plan is to bankrupt the NYS retirement system with retired cops because so many of my fellow officers are healthy and living long, active, amazing lives well into their nineties. I want them to empty their buckets and live for another twenty years. All of them. I want to help them get rid of all the shit that has happened to them and is still buried deep inside. The only successful way to accomplish this is to help each other, train everyone, and give them the knowledge about how to take care of their own. Not relying on government, not the administration, but each other. One day soon this stigma will be annihilated because there will be more of us that have gotten the help we needed than the ones still holding on to the old school mentality of stigma and negativity. For those of you that won't buy in to what I'm saying, how's that working out for you?

I want officers to get regular appointments with a therapist, not just get a physical exam every year. We have to save ourselves or everyone in LE will experience the same downward spiral eventually. If it can happen to someone like Joe, and someone like me, it can happen to anyone. We are all told to go for an annual physical, yet nobody says to go get your head checked along with it. What I've learned is that the mind and body work together, when one isn't working it has a direct effect on the other. Many studies have been conducted and many books written on this very topic. I am urging all of you, go make a therapy appointment with a culturally competent clinician who understands our culture. Don't be afraid to be human. I can tell you first hand that your physical and mental condition will be greatly improved once those pebbles are dumped out of that bucket.

NYLEAP also provides education so that signs and symptoms of Cumulative Career Traumatic Stress (CCTS) do not go unnoticed and, when noticed, the stigma that goes with getting mental health assistance is broken. It's okay to need help. We have been training peers all over NYS and have trained almost 2,000 to date. That's an impressive number but it's also just a drop in the bucket. I want every officer nationwide to have this knowledge and I won't stop until they do. That's a big goal. BIG. You already know about the cultural constraints.

I brought LEAP to New York, but cannot take credit for the program itself. In 2014, my younger brother Mike, in the Virginia State Police, was part of their Critical Incident Stress Management (CISM) team. He attended a PCIS where Dr. Eric Skidmore was speaking. Mike had a good conversation with the Doctor afterwards and told him about me and what I was doing in New York. We made contact and I started gaining knowledge by looking into his theories and methods. All of this was done on my own time, with my own money. After I had attended several seminars for observational purposes, I went to one as a participant. It was heavy and cathartic. I was a believer.

Dr. Eric Skidmore is the 'Godfather' of the Law Enforcement Assistance Program, (LEAP). He was hired by the South Carolina Law Enforcement Division(SLED) to create the LEAP program in 1997. He is best known for modifying the FBI version of Post Critical Incident Seminars (PCIS) and trademarking his LE specific version. All organizations must have his permission to follow the format; he did this because the format *works*. It is a strict model and must be maintained in order for it to be effective. It is remarkably effective. It also eliminates the possibility of competing entities hosting different versions of the PCIS. This was a brilliant idea in my opinion and maintains the integrity of the model.

Ms. Beverly Coates was his assistant during the development and for the next twenty-five years. Her son, Mark Hunter Coates, was murdered during a traffic stop on Interstate 95 in 1992, one of the first ever shootings caught on camera. That tape is shown at many Academies all over the nation. She contributed immensely to the success of these programs and worked up to her death in January of 2023. Her presence and energy are greatly missed.

After my PCIS participation and catharsis, I was determined to bring this program to New York State, so on my own dime I applied for the 501c3 non-profit status. Dr. Skidmore and I decided to team up on the project. I was honored; at that time there were just a couple of state LEAP Programs, now there are sixteen. We brought peers from South Carolina, North Carolina, Georgia, and Virginia north and pulled off the first three-day seminar in Buffalo in 2019. We had to start somewhere so I paid five thousand dollars on my own credit card for the meeting space and the hotel rooms. I didn't care; I had accomplished my mission. NYLEAP took hold. I walked out of there saying, "This was the most amazing thing in the world, but I cannot afford it! Not on a cop's salary!" I was overjoyed. Now, in 2023, New York, South Carolina, Virginia and North Carolina work together to assist other states with the initiation of their programs; we call it a jump-start and I'm incredibly proud to work with the men and women of LEAP to get these other states up and running.

Post Critical Incident Seminars (PCIS) are three-day peer to peer programs working with professional clinical support. There are five clinicians, and all attendees have a private session before they leave. If I told you I brought thirty officers into a room and we set the tone so that they are able to express themselves and talk about the hardest times of their lives, you might not believe me, but it happens. Andy Carrier makes it happen. We go all around the table and everyone tells us why they are there. As human beings, sometimes we don't know what or why certain things stick with you. There may be a trigger, an event, that triggers another trigger.

The schedule is always the same; we 'break down' the attendees on Monday, get them sharing and get them comfortable. Then they are all assigned to small groups, and that's where the magic happens. They start healing each other. That's where the catharsis comes from. By the time Wednesday comes, there is a difference in their gate, their appearance. There has generally been a weight lifted and if their buckets aren't empty, they are a hell of a lot lighter. It's incredible and it's a great start to their personal journey of wellness. They know that they've been to the depths of hell and now they can lean on each other. We provide a family. They will never be alone again. It's incredible. We do seven of those seminars a year in New York. Did I say it was incredible? I know I did. That's not a typo. It's incredible, amazing and all of those other words. We help our fellow officers live better, longer, healthier lives. The LEAP programs are open to anyone who needs help, regardless of the officer's home state.

LEAP is the only entity that I know of which includes, welcomes, and encourages spouses of the participants to attend. This is a very important point. When the spouses attend and see what we see, we can save even more marriages. Spouse peers are an equally essential and integral part of our program. They understand and teach why partners are the way they are. As we have talked about, officers go through phases in their career. They spend more time on the job than they do at home in many cases; they become their job. Often, that means a lot of changes when they come home from work and a lot of pressure for the spouse to relate, accept and understand what they are going through. Even tougher is that fact that the officer doesn't often talk about work, mostly in an effort to protect the family from that horror. Listen guys and gals, give your significant other much more credit than that! Spouses can help carry the weight of those pebble buckets, help empty that bucket and identify when their partner needs help if they have the knowledge to do so. Marriage is a team effort, just like law enforcement. Had I followed these simple things and included my spouse in my struggle, I might still be married today. I know for a fact that I won't ever again treat someone I love the way I treated her. I hope to have nothing less than a healthy relationship moving forward. We simply have to do a better job with our relationships, and have open communication. Often times I've had a partner tell me at a PCIS that they had never heard their spouse talk about any of the things they brought up during the seminar, and that they had no idea what had happened to them on the job. It's that light bulb effect again, and I love seeing it. It brings them closer together and sheds light on what was once a very dark area.

We bring the spouses in and train them the same way we teach our peers. What to look for, what to see, what to do. They need to be confident that they can help and should help. Instead of watching their spouse (or someone else's) deteriorate, we supply them with the knowledge to manifest change. The divorce rate of LE officers is far higher than the national average; that is just one more statistic our programs would like to improve. When officers isolate and lose connection to their co-workers and their spouses, the bucket is full and bad shit happens.

Another LEAP program, Traumatic Loss Seminar (TLS) is a four day event and again I was able to attend both as an observer and as a participant. Again, I was very impressed, and can tell you firsthand that these programs work. They certainly worked for me; cathartic, is the perfect description of what happens; the programs helped me heal using Thanatology. This particular seminar is taught only by South Carolina LEAP at this time. TLS focuses on responders that have had a sudden loss; it can be their partner, another officer or even a family member.

Thanatology is a science dedicated to better understanding death, dying, grief, loss and bereavement. TLS brings in a truly recognized expert in the field of Thanatology, Dr. Therese Rando. The field utilizes a wide variety of theory and practices to help people cope with loss of life. Dr. Rando's organization is based in Rhode Island,

and is world renowned on the complicated subject of grief. She is the Clinical Director of TLS programs in SC, and we've been thrilled to have her teach at PCIS in New York. Dr. Rando is remarkable; she can break down grief and loss and make the victim understand what's happening, what's making them feel the way they feel. It's phenomenal. She digs into it, describes the impacts and feelings of grief and then normalizes it. Most importantly, she offers people a path to move forward and understand the phases.

Some thanatology literature and theory indicate that grief is a progression, one step after the other. However, Dr. Rando found that in her research; the pain is not necessarily linear, and she has proven that the stages of grief do not always occur in the same order. As I certainly experienced with my own family, it's very different for everyone. She has a great way of helping us understand that everyone, sooner or later, faces the same losses. Her internationally recognized books on coping and grieving have changed how many people think the grieving process occurs. We are beyond pleased that she is a part of the LEAP programs; one of her current studies is the interface between posttraumatic stress and grief as well as self-help after traumatic loss. Dr. Rando is definitely a hero of mine. She has helped an incredible number of people heal, including me, and I consider her a friend.

LEAP is a predominantly volunteer organization; I pay the clinicians but not the presenters or peers. I have gathered some of the most amazing people in the world; they are my family. They have all been touched by trauma in their professional and personal lives, everybody has a story, most of us more than one, and everyone is incredibly committed to the program. Each state LEAP organization is independent, each is funded differently; the main standardization is the class and seminar structure, which has to happen to be called a LEAP program. Other states have instituted similar programs, so the peer concept is truly spreading across the nation.

At the beginning of NYLEAP we would host trainings with just four or five people; it was still absolutely worthwhile. Some were there just for a day off, honestly. Or that's what they told their peers. As I've said over and over, as officers we were taught, and more importantly told, not to admit that we needed help. There wasn't a lot of buy-in. Now, we have a waiting list for all these classes. We do one a month at least, sometimes more. We are funded by an assortment of entities, and of course it never seems to be enough. Some money is private, some comes from NYDCJS. We do seminars however and whenever we can find the money and the place and the time. I am desperately looking for a line item in the NY State budget. I feel that there are lots of items in that budget that are much less important than this. Our class size is now generally thirty to forty, with as many as fifty attendees. There is certainly a tremendous need.

LEAP members now train peers nationwide with our format. I taught in California last year; it's very rewarding to see it taking off. The goal is to train every LE officer as a peer. If they can't provide the support themselves, then at least they can direct someone who asks for help to the resources that they need. That's a lot of people to connect a lot of people and save a lot of lives. The potential is incredible. Personally, I speak and interview everywhere and anywhere I get the opportunity, radio shows, television, assorted associations across the nation. If the event will help spread the word about what I am trying to accomplish, I do my absolute best to make it happen.

In May of 2023 I addressed the Southern Tier Law Enforcement Memorial Association here in New York State. The more I connect with these LE groups the more support we all get, emotionally and monetarily. A lot of my job is awareness outside law enforcement too; it's up to all of us to be honest and let the public know that we need their support, again, both emotionally and monetarily. A prominent attorney in Western New York approached me after my speaking engagement. "I'm very impressed," he told me. "I need you to know you're polished. I didn't expect that from an officer." Quite a compliment, if just a little bit backhanded. He went on to tell me that his father works in the corporate world, on very similar problems. Humanity everywhere encounters similar stresses and traumas; people aren't always ready to admit they need help, but sooner or later everyone does, in one form or another. This particular speaking engagement led to an extensive story on the Binghamton Channel 10 Evening News. The tag line for that interview is "Local County Working to Break the Stigma to Stop Police Suicides." That headline indicates I definitely got our message across, and that always makes the long drives and long hours worthwhile.

We give our law enforcement protective gear but we don't protect their minds; I call it psychological armor. It's the component that's missing at the academies and throughout our career. A first line supervisor is perhaps the hardest job in law enforcement. Generally the rank of Sergeant, these administrators get pressure from above and from those below them. They deal with the officers one on one and can often recognize the changes and see the potential problems. First line supervisors are the meat in the sandwich; I believe they are the untapped resource in peer support because they see it all. If an officer is going through something and things change in their baseline, then the sergeant will be the first to notice it. Sergeants see the changes from day to day. For example, if an officer is normally out there writing tons of tickets, making a lot of arrests consistently, is always on time for work, and their uniform and gear are always squared away, then this is what we come to expect from that person. If several of those things start to change drastically then this will be noticed by the sergeant. They are the ones who correct the paperwork, see the monthly performance stats, etc.

The old school mentality would be to first talk with the officer and make them aware that if their deficiencies are not corrected there would be a move toward discipline. It's the way it's always been handled. When an officer is experiencing stress either from work or at home it effects their performance adversely, just like it did to me. Adding disciplinary action on top of what they are already distressed about is certainly not going to help them; it will only add to their stress.

What I've found to be very effective is to add intervention from peer support *before* a situation moves to discipline. Every agency in the world should put this into place. This will give the officer a chance to face whatever issue they are experiencing head on and deal with it. The trained peer support officer will be able to delve deeply into what is affecting the troubled officer and show them ways to deal with it; if it's too deep for the peer support officer then they will be able to direct them to a higher level of care. I've seen firsthand the benefits of this taking place, not only in my agency but agencies all over that I have trained. It's really perfect in its simplicity because I assure you I've never heard a struggling officer go in and thank their admin for disciplining them when what they really needed was a little help and guidance. Discipline will only drive them further down the rabbit hole. It's two-fold positive because not only have you corrected the problem without discipline, but you have boosted the morale of the agency. That positive benefit will be seen by other officers and we all know how cops talk; they will know and understand that someone has their back on this job and will step in to help. First line supervisors are undoubtedly crucial to the chain of events that can save the next suicide.

New York is currently the only state that has an Administrative Level PCIS; I initiated that in the fall of 2022. It's very important that LE administrators go specifically to their own class because they can be more open and honest among themselves rather than mixing ranks. Officers encounter a different set of issues at different levels of command; different levels make different decisions. At first it was very stressful, but what we reinforced was that we understand their jobs are tough because they get pressures, unique pressures, from the top and the bottom. I found that creating a seminar environment including only their direct peers made a huge difference. When their subordinates were present, they could not open up and share their burdens. Again, the key is peer support. People will open up to their equals. We had a second seminar in January for the rank of Lieutenant or above, it was well attended and successful. We now have requests to host another one and I have received calls from many other states wishing to send some of their admin to us. We will host it as often as we can and be honored to have admin from all of the country once again.

LEAP and the other programs are putting their best foot forward and making it happen. We are teaching and training as often as we can; for two years we've had a wait list to get into our programs. When I started talking about this stuff, I was astonished to learn one in four people think of suicide at some point in their life. I believe it happens even more frequently in law enforcement. When I started this crusade, I was told that my ideas wouldn't work, that I shouldn't do this. My fellow officers laughed at me, literally. Literally, laughed. I was going against a culture that didn't, and in some cases still doesn't, want to hear what I am saying. I'm still talking. And now, they've started listening.

The younger generation, thankfully, is more likely to reach out, which is why LEAP has social media platforms in place with messages that we hope are impactful. My favorite recent quote that we shared? "I don't know how my story will end, but nowhere in my text will ever read…*I gave up.*" Here at LEAP, we understand and respect how hard it can be to take that first step. We'll be with you for all the other steps, too. Promise.

I want to bring this concept, these programs, nationwide. I *will* bring this nationwide. Every state should have these programs available; access to PCIS are key to the sanity of the people on the front line. We have begun; see us on www.US-LEAP.org. I hope and pray that we can get federal funding moving forward. We are currently applying for a federal level 501c3, non-profit status. Once established, we can and we will go forward with speaking to Congressional Members to support these programs. We have considerable support already, and since this is not a partisan issue, this is a human issue, I see it as a slam-dunk as soon as we can get it in front of Congress. They wouldn't dare turn it down. We are losing officers at an exponential rate through both suicide and attrition, and people are seeing the result of that. If Congress can see this as a solution and that the alternative is not having protection, they must do it. We have to save everyone, both sides of the aisle, both sides of the issues.

I was working on this book and received a text from an officer that attended a seminar not long ago. That text was all praise and I live for those! It means I'm making a difference. It means that our programs work, and I am proud to tell you that is just one message of many that I have received over the years. We've saved lives in more ways than one. It's huge. It's addicting. I can't get enough of it. I've been very fortunate to connect with some great people along the way. My Blue Family has been extended in ways I never imagined.

With all that said, I want to make you aware that not all peer programs are beneficial. In the past several years there have been a lot of pop up peer programs making many claims of help and success. I've found many of them to be looking for a way to make some quick money and benefit themselves while not really working for the benefit of the first responders. Programs should be vetted, and NYLEAP along with Valor Station are fully transparent; we have nothing to hide and put first responders first without worrying about money. One of my colleagues talks about snake oil salesmen, and he's one hundred percent spot on. Just because there is a program out there, doesn't mean it's a good program. Do your homework and make sure they have your best intentions in mind before jumping in with them.

ADVANCING THE TREATMENTS, PERFECTING THE PROGRAM

As we've discussed, and as we all know, there are many things in life that you can't control. Wasting time and energy focusing on them will only bring you down. It's important to stay focused on the things in your life that you do have control over and the first thing is yourself. We MUST make it okay for officers to get the help and support they need. When I do a class it's all about inclusion because we cannot lean on the government or our administrators. I teach people what to look for. We *must* take care of each other. We are providing the help that they need confidentially, and we must also change the culture so that it doesn't need to be a secret. It doesn't need to be embarrassing or scary to admit that you saw some shitty thing that someone did to someone else and it affected you! That's okay. It's human. And we're still all human. "It's okay to not be okay."

While there are many people who have assisted me along this path, there is one person I must mention in regard to peer support within my agency. Lieutenant Peter Difiore is my confidential supervisor here in Warren County. He has been my oversight since the program began and without him and without his level of confidentiality, my program would not have been successful. He reminds me of my brother in many ways and is always looking to take care of his fellow officers, his people, always working behind the scenes to make sure they have what they need. He has helped me on many occasions when I needed to get someone into treatment or connected with local resources by assisting me administratively and making sure officer's schedules are adjusted or modified so they could get what they needed to continue being functional at work. His efforts should not go unnoticed and if there were a way to clone Lieutenant Difiore and put him in every LE agency in the world, I guarantee the morale would increase and the numbers of suicide, depression, alcoholism, and divorce rates would be significantly lower almost immediately. That is the caliber of person he is and what he brings to this job. In so many cases, these are the heroes that I am working with. This man, and many like him, have advanced our cause, one case at a time. I'm proud and honored to call Lt. Difiore my Brother.

As human beings, we are all incredibly complicated. As I saw firsthand with my family, and have learned more and more about since, everyone grieves differently. Everyone handles stresses and traumas differently, heals at different rates and fills their buckets at different rates. Some veteran officers may have a giant bucket of pebbles and can handle it pretty well, others may need support at a much earlier time in their careers. The mind can hide away things that we don't even remember on a conscious level. Very often, clinical depression is involved as well. LEAP utilizes specifically chosen specialists and clinicians who understand what law enforcement goes through. The huge majority of our people are veterans of one or more military or law enforcement organizations who have then gone into psychological work for the very same reason I am doing what I'm doing. Clearly, there is a need.

We've made a lot of headway but peer support programs are still not standardized, not as readily available as I would like them to be. Law enforcement has what we call Accredited Organizations, which means the agency is doing things at the highest level. Our agency here in Warren County is accredited. The recommendations and requirements are determined by a board. The board passed a rule in 2022 that any accredited agency needs to implement a mental health wellness program. The government finally said, *yes, we need this*. It is another huge step toward our goal.

●●

We talked about Dr. Therese Rando and the work she has done with grief therapy. Her team also delves into a therapy that LEAP has found incredibly effective as well as interesting. This cutting edge process is called EDMR, Eye Movement Desensitization and Reprocessing. EMDR was developed by Dr. Francine Shapiro in 1989 and is defined by Cleveland Clinic as "a mental health treatment technique that involves moving your eyes in a specific way while you process traumatic memories." The goal is to help people heal from trauma or other distressing life experiences. Memories that have been adequately processed can be remembered without being relived or emotionally activated.

As part of my participation in TLS and PCIS I have experienced EDMR therapy and want to share the experience with you. In addition, I have read numerous case studies and seen countless examples of people who have successfully undergone this seemingly unconventional treatment. Before I underwent EMDR, it was very difficult for me to speak about Joe, very visceral, tremendously painful. Whenever I would talk about it I had an actual physical reaction. Through the process of EMDR, the visceral effect was lessened considerably; the level of anxiety and stress went away after this process. Bad things can get locked in the wrong place in the brain; law enforcement tends to have trouble with a lack of REM sleep, and these incidents get filed in hidden places. There is no time to accept and process traumas. The EMDR program takes those files, those memories, and manages them. It does not take these experiences away, nothing can, but it lets you control how they affect you.

During the process itself, you can feel something going on but you don't understand it. "How the fuck do I feel better?" I kept asking myself. It seemed like a five hundred pound weight had been lifted off my shoulders. I physically felt different; the experience, the process, had peeled that layer of stress off of me. I came across several scientific explanations of how EMDR works, from slowing down the overstimulated amygdala (emotional center) in the brain to synchronizing brain waves to activating both hemispheres through bilateral stimulation. Unlike treatments that focus on directly altering emotions, thoughts and responses resulting from traumatic experiences, EMDR focuses directly on the memory and is intended to change the way that memory is stored in the brain, thus reducing and eliminating the problematic symptoms. According to the Cleveland Clinic Website, "...you reprocess what you remember from the negative events. That reprocessing helps 'repair' the mental injury from that memory." This results in a new acceptance of your reality, that's how I see it. Although this concept is an amazing mystery to me, I know it worked in my case.

EMDR therapies can take several weeks in a clinical setting; the average seems to be six to twelve sessions. In our PCIS, we offer a variation in one session that can be very successful if the person is ready to heal and understands the source of their pain. I have seen officers walk out of those sessions just as I described myself, a weight lifted off their shoulders. They literally walk taller, prouder, perhaps more like a younger version of themselves. It is one of my favorite transformations to observe.

NYLEAP is trying to use the most effective methods available and we understand that no one process will work for all individuals, but we are always willing to try! Contact us and we will definitely do our best. One Iraq war veteran had a similar reaction to my own. He inquired emphatically, after his EMDR, "I'm trying to ask you, how did you do that? That pit in my chest is not there. God, it's not there. This was all I had to do for the last four years? This is different, I don't feel heavy...I feel different about it. I kept thinking that EMDR won't work ...(in my case)...I really didn't let those guys down. I'm not God. I wish I could have saved them but ...It's okay..." from www.apa.org/PTSD Clinical Practice Guidelines.

We have touched on the crucial concept of Peer Support and offering resolution rather than discipline. That is cultural and has to be done on all levels. Now that our PCIS programs and other programs have a waiting list; that's huge. It means that many arms of law enforcement are trying my methods.

If you are early in your career or reading this as a part of your training, someone that gave you this book cares about you. Treat this information like you would the most important information given to you during your training. Use it to help yourself and to help your brothers and sisters throughout this career. Law enforcement can be one of the most rewarding careers available if you keep yourself healthy; you are helping people.

To those of you who are halfway through or close to the end of your journey in this career, I hope it will inspire you to take a look at yourself, and think about the things discussed here. Ask yourself, 'am I the same person I was before I started this job?' If the answer is no, you might have some work to do before exiting this career so that you may live a long and happy life and collect as much of that well-deserved retirement. You earned every penny with your blood, sweat, and tears. Put the time and effort in to help yourself and to be the best version of yourself because your loved ones deserve the best version of you. You're a hero.

If you are in the Academy and reading this, please take this information and use it to maintain yourself and have a healthy career because there's one thing nobody can take away from you and that is knowledge. If you are well within your career and can identify with some of the things that I've talked about in this book, please reflect upon yourself. Get that bucket cleaned out before you retire so that you'll be able to enjoy the rest of your life and leave the badge behind.

This career is a huge responsibility, to uphold what's right, to uphold the laws of this great nation. It can give you purpose and a reason to thrive in your life or it can take everything from you. Only you have the power to make that decision for yourself.

www.NYLEAP.org

VALOR STATION

I'm starting a treatment facility. That's a big statement isn't it? We are, really, I cannot take full credit but let me tell you my excitement knows no bounds on the potential of Valor Station, a twenty-two bed Intensive Out Patient (IOP) facility. I want to thank Dr. Matthew Carpenter, the Vice President of NYLEAP, Andrew Carrier, the Clinical Director and Chief Operating Officer(COO), as well as Cliff Richards, Chief Executive Officer(CEO) of Valor Station.

Andy Carrier is a retired Captain from the Georgia State Patrol who became a clinician. He has been the Clinical Director for NYLEAP since its inception. I have mentioned him before and Andy is able to connect with other Law Enforcement on an amazing level. He knows the job because he's been doing it successfully for over thirty years. Adding the clinical aspect and now treating officers was just the icing on the cake. I've watched so many officers come out of an EMDR session with Andy smiling and walking on air. He simply connects well and is a perfect fit for this endeavor. He and Cliff brought me in to Valor Station after the vision started to take shape and I am forever grateful to be a part of what we are building.

Dr. Matthew Carpenter has suffered the loss of far too many co-workers to suicide and knows what this career can do to you. He is a police officer with the City of Rochester, New York and holds a Doctorate degree. He has been my backbone for the past few years working alongside me on this mission. His devotion, strength, and courage has helped me not only with NYLEAP but in my personal life as well. He shares my vision and also my tenacity to do whatever it takes to assist officers in need.

■■

Cliff Richards has run the Hale Foundation in Augusta, Georgia for many years in the addiction field. Cliff has carried the torch for Valor Station and saw the need to develop it as he was touched by the stories of trauma and addiction in relation to LE all over the country. Cliff has been working alongside us for the past few years and has developed a love, passion and, earnest care for the Law Enforcement community nationwide. Without Cliff, none of this would have been possible and officers all over the Country will have him to thank for many years to come. Cliff is a lot like me when it comes to passion for helping our cops. His tenacity and fervor inspire our team like nothing else. He never had to take this on, yet he has done so with incredible zeal.

It will be an honor to work alongside these fine gentlemen for many years to come. It's like a dream come true, where we all get to work together and share the same vision and goal; getting and keeping our officers healthy on the beat, letting them know that it's not a sign of weakness to ask for and accept help, it is a sign of strength.

We have discovered problems within our culture, including first responders and the military and are bringing those to light. More importantly, we can now help solve the problem. Valor Station is a program for cops to understand that they have a place to go. If you need help, you get it, no strings. Just show up, and then it's your responsibility to mentor others. Peer Support. This will be a First Responder Exclusive facility; you need to be a first responder to attend. We have designed it to cater to the needs of first responders without having to worry about anything from outside cultures. You can heal with your brothers and sisters in blue and from branches of the military.

The staff will be comprised of former first responders as well to add an additional layer of camaraderie. The non-profit aspect will allow us to kick off a capital campaign nationwide so that we can raise money to cover the costs of treatment for any first responder that can't afford it or doesn't have insurance benefits to cover it. That won't be an easy task on our part, but I'm certain when the word gets out about what we are doing for our nation's heroes, the support will be overwhelming. Please help us spread the word!

We desperately need dedicated First Responders in this proud nation. Let's work together to get and keep them healthy so that when you call 911 in *your* time of need, they will be there to help you and your family. If anyone out there reading this has any great knowledge on fundraising, or knows of any grants or has benefactors looking to support our Nation's First Responders, **please** reach out to me personally.

This project has been in the works for over two years and received official non-profit 501c3 status in April of 2023. Our social media is already in place and teams are ready to move down to Augusta, Georgia to make it happen. These dedicated people are going to uproot themselves and their families and move to Georgia because they know we are at a critical point with our law enforcement services nationwide. There are too many suicides and too much unhappiness. We are going to help bring the hero status back to law enforcement, one person at a time. We are truly going to help first responders overcome the effects of traumas that they experience every day.

This facility is not only for LE members, but military as well. We welcome them. There is a tremendous amount of trauma on military bases around the world that we never hear about. If you would like to read another excellent example of trauma and suicidal thoughts turned into helping others, look up the book *Knot Today* by Scott W.F. Aubin. Scott works with NYLEAP on a regular basis presenting at PCIS meetings and has a hell of a story, just like the rest of us. Everybody has a story. We must not disregard or underestimate that. Needing help is never a weakness. When we get this culture changed, asking for support will no longer lead to failure or rejection or a stigma that you cannot shake.

■■

Our law enforcement officers are so blinded by the culture of keeping things in they are taking their own lives. I ask every seminar participant this question; 'Are you the same person you were when you took the oath?" I don't think I've ever gotten a positive response. That really pisses them off, and of course much more importantly makes them think. Most LE never wanted to admit I was creating a program that is necessary. Now they are saying, "Oh shit, I'm *not* the same person I was. I'm *not*. It's okay, our jobs change us. All of us." The culture will make even good guys into these assholes that I've run across my whole career. That's the culture that we are trying to break. The stigma. The people that I have gathered work with us now are the ones that resisted the culture, became clinicians and therapists and they get it. We don't want this cream of the crop to become cynical, angry and volatile officers that need help the most.

Valor Station. Remember the name, remember the mission.

www.ValorStation.com

THE SAME DREAM

We, as law enforcement, must do better. Our culture nearly drove me insane, nearly drove me to suicide; now you know my story. Joe's own people betrayed him, the ultimate betrayal, because it came from within. He had nowhere to turn, and stood up for what he thought was right, only to be taken down by a culture that doesn't always do the right thing, a culture that, for the most part, is stuck in a very deep rut. Joe knew we needed to do better.

A law enforcement badge portrays our position and authority along with the willingness to sacrifice one's safety to assist others. Our badge is a symbol and a promise to uphold the best interests of the community in which we serve. Members of the Boston Police Force were exonerated from stealing; they were found innocent by our legal system because it had always been done that way. The Police in Boston reportedly lied regularly on their timesheets. Their superiors knew it, and most officers reportedly followed suit. That's fucked up. We haven't heard about the officers who were innocent of that, and I'm sure there were many that refused the practice. I'm just using them as an example, I'm not picking them out of a lineup. Regardless, as a group, law enforcement has to stop doing those sorts of things; we must stop following leaders and other officers that should not be followed. We must. It reflects badly on all of us, all contingents of first responders. All of us. One step, one officer, one incident at a time, we can change this culture. We *are* changing this culture. Just because we've always done things this way doesn't mean it's the right way to do it.

My brother took the road less traveled; he chose not to follow the majority and he was punished rather than heralded. My brother wanted to be the best, we all want to be the best, and that's not just law enforcement. I still believe that, deep down, humanity is inherently good. I truly want to believe that, so I do. I've seen, firsthand, some ridiculously shitty things done by people to other people. We all have. I'm not saying I can explain that, and I'm not saying that those perpetrators shouldn't be incarcerated. They made bad choices. They broke the law. In that case, punishment is the appropriate repercussion.

Law enforcement officers can make the same bad choices that other people do, but it is magnified by the media, and, frankly, by the fact that we are supposed to *protect and serve,* we are supposed to be exemplary. Situations get out of hand and sometimes someone gets hurt. When it's the police that get out of hand, it is often because they have not had the time or opportunity to recover from multiple traumas, and then we all pay the price. Law enforcement is now looked down upon rather than placed on a pedestal as it was when Joey started, as it was when I started twenty-five years ago. We used to be heroes. A lot has changed, and now we need to change, too. We need to be accountable, held responsible, both for our actions and for taking care of our people so they are not driven to the brink of insanity by what they see and the choices they are forced to make. The best way to do this is by sharing my experience with every first responder in the world.

It's not right, to judge all of law enforcement by the actions of a few. However, we cannot blame the public. We have to try and help those of us who, on their next traffic stop, with their bucket too full of stones and pebbles from this job, might use too much force. Or pull out their weapon because they feel threatened by a public who no longer appreciates the risks that LE takes every day. Every day. Remember the ninety percent boredom and then the ten percent blinding fear and wondering what the fuck could possibly happen next? There's a great line from a movie that says, "I saw a bullet with my name on it today. I'm still here." There can be happy endings. There are many happy endings.

Let's talk about the concept of intervention rather than discipline. Old school methods of management believed in discipline rather than asking why. That doesn't cure the problem, it doesn't cure the underlying issue. We are now offering, encouraging, and preferring intervention techniques. We ask how we got to where we are, then we can get to the root of the problem and provide the tools to repair the damage. We need to empty that guy's bucket, and give that officer a chance to recover without discipline first. Look what happened to Joe when he was questionably disciplined. Departments can save lives as well as money, time, stress, all the other shit that goes along with bad choices. We need to offer these resources to everyone. We need to continue finding better solutions. Our people are fried to a crisp, they hate their life and everyone around them. If we offer them help first instead of running right to discipline as we've always done in the past, we offer them a chance to correct the issue with peer support and it never leads to disciplinary action. Again, this way will save time, money and increase the morale in any agency.

Some people think I'm crazy for working full-time, running NYLEAP, venturing out and starting a treatment facility for first responders, starting a nationwide nonprofit to benefit all law enforcement by spreading knowledge and training our people how to survive in this career, and even better to *thrive* in this career. I will agree that I burn the candle at both ends. I have dedicated my life to this mission, the mission of making this job better than I found it, and by spreading the knowledge that I have gained so that others won't suffer in silence any longer. I hope to continue this work until the day I die; by that time my tank will be empty with the wheels falling off, nothing left to give. That's the way I want to go out of this world; those are my terms and I have made that decision, I have made that choice.

I am very uncomfortable receiving awards or accolades for doing what I do. I feel strongly that this is what we should, as human beings, be doing, so why would I be recognized for simply doing what we all need to be doing? The biggest rewards I receive are seeing someone that my team has helped pay it forward to help another. That is the key. If people don't get support they turn to options that cannot be undone.

When my brother took his life mine fell apart. Lots of lives fell apart. As law enforcement, we walk the *Thin Blue Line.* The line between absolute chaos and peace. Peace within is as important as keeping the peace. It's not an easy job. It's a fucking hard job. We need to make choices that will lead to the least amount of violence, chaos and pain. For everyone. Soon the believers are going to outnumber the non-believers. We've got to start taking better care of each other. We've got to change police culture.

We are starting to do our best to take care of our people, it's that simple. If we don't do it, the entire system will fail. We can modify our culture so that there are more happy endings. That was Joey's dream, to help create a better force, to teach people to make better choices. His dream was to leave this job better than he found it.

My goal and my dream is that every office in the world has this book on their shelf; that it's part of what they teach their new recruits. I want to make it part of the curriculum of every police academy nationwide. I want to be a positive force, I want to teach our people how to do better, as well as be healthier and happier, to live longer lives. By teaching our recruits about this aspect of law enforcement, we are giving them psychological body armor that they can use to sustain a successful and fulfilling career, resulting in a long retirement without the baggage and negativity from their responsibilities following them.

This goal is a tremendous, continuous motivator because I know what can ultimately happen. It is incredibly obvious that our Peer Support Programs are effective; obvious not only to our agencies as a whole but to individual officers all over the nation. They are recommending us to each other, and there is no better recommendation than that.

Law enforcement just needed a little bit of hope. We just needed someone to help us, another peer, to make sure we knew we weren't alone. To have our back. We at LEAP do have their back and your back. We protect confidentiality, we take everyone from start to finish. We don't leave anybody behind. We give them the best service possible; we give them hope.

As a proud nation, we expect the best from our police officers, our officers need support and it is now happening. As I write this, and as you read this, these programs are gaining momentum and the pieces are falling into place thanks to a dedicated group of veterans and officers. From the PCIS classes to Valor Station, the resources are out there. Use them. If you need to use them, use them. And then pass the information along. Be a part of the solution, not the problem. If you read this and felt that a light bulb or two went off in your head, don't ignore it. Most cops will read this and say "that's me" but never do anything about it. Please have the courage to understand why you are feeling and acting the way you are and then most importantly, take my advice and do some work on yourself. We deserve to have a higher quality of life. We deserve the same happiness and contentment often seen in non-LE folks. We deserve to live longer than fifty seven.

From an officer safety standpoint think about this. Would you rather go into a life or death situation with another officer who has gotten help and been in therapy working on themselves, an officer with a clear head and focused on the situation. Or would you rather take the chance of going into that same situation with someone who doesn't have a clear head and is dealing with unresolved issues, quite possibly making a bad choice in a split second where your life is on the line. My choice is clear, I want the Officer who has already gotten help. Everyone knows what it's like to have a lot going on in your head, especially when you're on the job and that's ok, just take care of it so you're the one everyone wants in that life or death situation. Pride is a wonderful thing, and I hope you are proud of the person you are, just don't let pride keep you from getting help if and when you need it. Pride has killed far too many officers to date, so don't let it get you too. We are trained to run into the gunfire not away from it and protect people we don't even know; you would do this in a heartbeat and not think twice. We all recognize that fact, so why wouldn't you have the strength and courage to reach out to your partner, your brothers and sisters in blue and ask them if they are ok? I'm asking you, begging you, have the courage to look after one another, because nobody else is doing it. We need to do a much better job of taking care of our own! Together we can do this. Together we can change this culture for the better. This is my story, and you have your own. I don't tell mine in the hopes of gaining sympathy, I tell it so that others can learn from it, hopefully it will help them see that there is a way out, a way to find themselves once again. The path may not be easy, but there is a way to look into the mirror and say "I recognize that person again." I'm proud to share it, and it's my gift to you. I'm proud of Joey, I'm honored to call him my brother, and without him none of this would have been possible. He's the true hero.

This book is a quick, impactful read that offers hope, insight, and resources, that will save lives. Pass it along. Give it to your spouse, put it in the breakroom at the station house. Give everyone else the knowledge you have gained from this. Through this book and these programs, the spirit of my brother lives on. Lieutenant Joseph J. Banish has saved, and improved, more lives than anyone would have imagined. His legacy lives on and I promise he has your back.

RESOURCES

www.NYLEAP.org
New York Law Enforcement Assistance Program
1 (518) 625-1899
YOU CAN REACH US ANYTIME.

■■

www.ValorStation.com

Taped April 15, 2020 www.LETRadioShow.com
Law Enforcement Today Radio Show

PCIS Seminar Audio Recording, NYLEAP, Watertown, New York, May 9, 2023

Boston Globe, electronic edition

World Population Review

www.CBSnews.com

www.ClevelandClinic.com

www.apa.org   PTSD Clinical Practice Guidelines

I have mentioned that other organizations have support programs in place. These are just a few examples, there are more and more reputable organization that have been implemented to assist.
Among them are:

International Critical Incident Stress Foundation ICISF

www.end-PTSD.org

www.Police1.com

**SEEKING HELP IS NOT
A SIGN OF WEAKNESS,
IT IS A SIGN OF STRENGTH.**

IF YOU NEED IT, DO IT.

IT'S OKAY NOT TO BE OKAY.

Made in the USA
Columbia, SC
04 November 2024